Panchayati Raj and Women Empowerment

Dependency versus Autonomy

Panchayati Raj and Women Empowerment

Dependency versus Autonomy

Nupur Tiwari
Faculty Member,
Rural Administration and Panchayati Raj,
Indian Institute of Public Administration (IIPA), New Delhi

New Century Publications
New Delhi, India

NEW CENTURY PUBLICATIONS
4800/24, Bharat Ram Road,
Ansari Road, Daryaganj,
New Delhi - 110 002 (India)

Tel.: 011-2324 7798, 4358 7398, 6539 6605
Fax: 011-4101 7798
E-mail: indiatax@vsnl.com • info@newcenturypublications.com
www.newcenturypublications.com

Editorial office:
LG–7, Aakarshan Bhawan,
4754-57/23, Ansari Road, Daryaganj,
New Delhi – 110 002

Tel.: 011-4356 0919

First Published: **July 2016**

ISBN: **978-81-7708-428-3**

Published by New Century Publications and printed at Salasar Imaging Systems, New Delhi.

Designs: Patch Creative Unit, New Delhi.

PRINTED IN INDIA

About the Book

Panchayats are local governments mandated in the Constitution of India. As per the Constitution, a three-tier structure of panchayats is in place across the country, excepting areas where Part IX of the Constitution does not apply. Panchayats are to be constituted, through elections every five years, except in States with a population of less than 20 lakh, where panchayats at two tiers may be created.

The Constitution recognizes the gram sabha, i.e. all the electors in a village panchayat. The Constitution provides that seats and offices of chairpersons be reserved for scheduled castes (SCs) and scheduled tribes (STs) in proportion to their respective population, and not less than one-third seats and offices of the chairpersons be reserved for women, including within the SC and ST reservations.

Women's increased political participation has yielded positive results. Issues central to the development—including health, nutrition, family income and education—have taken centre stage as women participate in panchayati raj institutions (PRIs), village development boards and other governance structures.

India has primarily relied upon the method of reservation to ensure women's presence in decision-making bodies. This has increased *de jure*, but not necessarily *de facto*, participation. There is a need to encourage women's participation in other kinds of groups and associations which contribute to an atmosphere of leadership by women.

About the Author

Dr. Nupur Tiwari is currently a Faculty Member, Rural Administration and Panchayati Raj at Indian Institute of Public Administration (IIPA), New Delhi. She has also served as faculty member at the Centre for Rural Studies, Lal Bhadur Shastri National Academy of Administration (LBSNAA), Mussoorie.

She has to her credit 35 research papers/articles published in national and international peer-reviewed journals. She has authored 3 books/monographs and contributed chapters in a number of books.

She was a member of the Thematic Group on Panchayati Raj and Local Self-government constituted by the Ministry of Development of North Eastern Region (DoNER). She was also involved in the Expert Committee for Leveraging Panchayati Raj, constituted by the Ministry of Panchayati Raj, Government of India.

Foreword

Democracy in India commences at the grassroots. We have close on 250,000 institutions of Constitutionally-sanctioned and Constitutionally-sanctified local self-government, to which we have elected 3.2 million representatives, a number nearly equal to the population of New Zealand or Norway or many Central American republics.

Of these, no less than a million are women in rural local self-government and another 200,000 in urban local bodies. There are more elected women in India alone than in the rest of the world put together. It is an achievement without precedent in history or parallel in the world.

We have secured such a large measure of women's representation in our local bodies primarily through the instrument of reservations—but not entirely so. For, whereas the reserved share of seats for women in our institutions of local self-government is 33 percent, the number of women actually elected is closer to 40 percent—for many women contest and win against male candidates from constituencies that are not reserved for women.

Indeed, in the State of Karnataka, it has been found that whereas the share of tribal women in seats reserved for tribals is 33 percent, in actual fact close to double that figure—some 65 percent—of the seats have been won by tribal women. The share for women belonging to the scheduled castes is 54 percent. Thus, it would appear that the hitherto most discriminated against section of the most discriminated against segments of Indian society have been the biggest gainers from the system of reservations. The fear of elite capture of these institutions has been effectively belied.

This large number of women from very traditional backgrounds emerge from the cloisters of their kitchens and closed family courtyards to knock on anonymous doors, walk the streets and argue from public platforms when they contest the elections. This initiation into public life empowers both the women who win and the women who lose—and even those women who watch their sisters contest and chose their representative from among the contestants.

Moreover, reservations for women in the Indian system of local self- government extend not only to seats in the local bodies but also to the office of president or chairperson. Thus, one-third of all such positions are reserved for women and give them high executive responsibility and experience. There are several instances of women getting elected to chair the local body even where the chair is not gender-reserved.

The criticism is sometimes made—and not always without foundation—that women candidates for reserved positions are proxies for their male relatives and that after the elections, the elected woman representative is rendered a rubber stamp with the dominant male relative—husband, father or brother—exercising effective power from behind—and often from even in front of—the stage.

There is no denying this, but to put matters in perspective we recently undertook a survey through one of our leading pollsters of some 20,000 elected representatives to ascertain the true picture of the performance of women in our local bodies[1]. It emerges from the survey that the proportion of elected women representatives (EWRs) from families with political antecedents in the village is really no greater than for males; the responses show a majority of women representatives are not proxies of their male relatives or patrons. As many as 58 percent of the women representatives are now taking their own decisions to contest elections. 60 percent of the women respondents said they faced no gender discrimination in their work. 60-64 percent said their interaction with local officials had significantly increased since their election. And as many as 94 percent said they found no

1. Study on Elected Women Representatives (EWRs) in Panchayati Raj Institutions (PRIs) (2008) based on a nationwide survey by AC Nielsen ORG-MARG, Ministry of Panchayati Raj, Government of India, New Delhi.

restrictions on their raising issues and making their comments in meetings of the local bodies and the Parliament of the people, that is, the *gram sabhas*. This, in turn, has led to the participation of women members in *gram sabha* meetings rising to as high as 68 percent to 78 percent. And, most heartening of all, a majority of the EWRs reported an enhancement in their personal effectiveness and image after being elected, both in the workplace and in the home.

It follows that gender specific programmes of training, skill development and capacity-building are necessary to more effectively equip women to play their due part in local self-government. This is where civil society and the intellectual community come into their own. They need to take upon themselves the burden of face-to-face training in small groups. The State, on the other hand, needs to harness the best of modern technology to reach such training and capacity-building electronically to women in every village and habitation of our vast country.

Our problems are complicated by the huge variety of languages in our country. As most women representatives are familiar with, and fluent in, only their respective languages or dialects, State governments and local NGOs have a major role to play in effectively communicating the substance and philosophy of local self-government to the elected representatives and, more especially, to the EWRs.

Further, as experience grows so also does independence of thought and action. Therefore, the single most important factor inhibiting the full exercise of power by elected women representatives is the reservation cycle; in most States, reserved seats for women are rotated every five years—if this were extended to a cycle of two or three terms, that is, ten or fifteen years, women who get re-elected in successive elections would tend to be more confident, more well-versed with their work and, therefore, more generally empowered than in a reservation cycle that lasts only a single term.

We also find that the self-help group movement is a

necessary and, indeed, vital supplement to the political empowerment of women through our local bodies as the movement economically empowers women both as individuals and as groups. The combination of economic empowerment through the self-help groups and political and social empowerment through the institutions of local self-government is changing the face of rural India. Half our population—the women of India—are emerging from millennia of subordination to men and contributing in the public domain to society at large what they have so far been confined to contributing to their children, families and home.

In consequence, social equations are changing within the family and in society at large. This is all to the good. For too long, half our national energies—the energies of our women—were locked up in the homestead. Now they are being deployed for the welfare and development of local communities. This is where gender-empowerment really matters for it is in communities and neighbourhoods that people live.

But the single most important factor which empowers women in our local bodies is the degree to which the local bodies themselves are empowered: the more these bodies are empowered, the more are the representatives in these bodies empowered; and, of course, the more the representatives are empowered, the more are the women elected representatives empowered.

While reservations and elections have indeed promoted the political and social empowerment of women in local self-governance, there is still a long way to go to secure the administrative and economic empowerment of women through the local bodies.

Mani Shankar Aiyar

Contents

Preface

Gender equality is a constituent of development as well as an instrument of development. No country can be deemed developed if half of its population is severely disadvantaged in terms of basic needs, livelihood options, access to knowledge, and political voice. It is an instrument of development because without gender equality, other goals of development will also be difficult to achieve, namely the goals of poverty alleviation, economic growth, environmental sustainability etc. A natural corollary of ensuring gender equality is the elimination of gender discrimination.

The socio-economic development of a country cannot be fully realized so long as its women are confined to subordinate position and their talents remain unexplored.

Advancement and empowerment of women has been a leading objective of state policy ever since the attainment of Independence in 1947. Institutions of different types—Central, State and Local Governments, non-governmental organisations (NGOs), civil society and other bodies—are active to ensure gender equality as laid down in the Constitution of India.

In the early years of the Independence, much of the country's governance was in the hands of elected representatives and the official machinery. Such a centralized approach did not produce desired results, especially in terms of the inclusion of marginalized groups within the governance processes. Constitutional, legislative and policy reforms since then and the continued administrative decentralization have increased the political participation of marginalized groups, especially poor women. Women's increased political participation has yielded positive results. Issues central to development—including health, nutrition, family income and education—have taken centre stage as women participate in panchayati raj institutions (PRIs), village development boards and other governance structures.

There has been growing acceptance of the importance to society of the full participation of women in decision-making and power at all levels and in all fora, including inter-governmental, governmental, and non-governmental sectors.

Panchayats are local governments mandated in the Constitution of India. As per the Constitution, a three-tier structure of panchayats is in place across the country, excepting areas where Part IX of the Constitution does not apply. Panchayats are to be constituted, through elections every five years, except in States with a population of less than 20 lakh, where panchayats at two tiers may be created.

There are nearly 2.5 lakh elected panchayats and 29 lakh elected representatives (ERs). The Constitution leaves it to the discretion of the States to devolve funds, functions and functionaries (3Fs) to the panchayats and States vary a great deal in the extent to which they have devolved powers to panchayats and equipped them with adequate manpower, infrastructure including office space and furniture, modern equipment, training etc., to enable them to perform their functions. An illustrative list of functions which can be devolved on the PRIs is given in Schedule XI of the Constitution.

The Constitution recognizes the gram sabha, i.e. all the electors in a village panchayat. The Constitution provides that seats and offices of chairpersons be reserved for the scheduled castes (SCs) and scheduled tribes (STs) in proportion of their respective population, and not less than one-third seats and offices of chairpersons be reserved for women, including within SC and ST reservations.

Article 243M of the Constitution, while exempting the Fifth Schedule areas from Part IX of the Constitution, provides that Parliament may by law extend its provisions to the scheduled and tribal areas subject to such exceptions and modifications as may be specified in such law and no such law shall be deemed to be an amendment to the Constitution. On the basis of the report of the Bhuria Committee submitted in 1995, the Parliament enacted the Panchayats (Extension to Scheduled Areas) Act, 1996 (PESA) to extend Part IX of the Constitution with certain modifications and exceptions to the Scheduled V areas of 9 States.

PESA envisages self-governance through the gram sabha, and, while extending the panchayati raj structure as envisaged in Part IX of the Constitution, gives wide powers to the gram sabhas in Schedule V areas.

PESA lays a framework of self-governance and people's control over resources through the gram sabhas in Schedule V areas. Yet, the implementation of PESA has not been satisfactory, partly because of the lack of interest shown by States to amend State laws in compliance with PESA provisions, but also because of the inadequacy of efforts to strengthen gram sabhas. Strengthening of panchayats and implementation of PESA in Schedule V areas has significant national importance as it can lead to improved governance and accountability in these areas.

Legislative enactments have dramatically increased women's access to decision-making structures in recent years. Many of the elected women entering the public arena for the first time lack confidence, feel isolated, and have no previous political experience. They need to develop their innate leadership skills. Studies conducted in different parts of the country show that 95 percent of the elected women representatives (EWRs) are first-timers in politics and join politics because that is what their male family/village members want. As first timers without previous exposure to politics, many of the elected women lack the capacity to function properly in the panchayats and municipalities, and consequently are not taken seriously by their colleagues. Sustained training and networking efforts are being undertaken both by government and non-government agencies to ensure that women's capacity to participate improves. With just a few years of experience, women have emerged as articulate, motivated leaders all over the country.

Constitutional provisions apart, there are complaints from various parts of the country regarding effective participation of women in local governance structures. Proxy politics, power brokering and gender discrimination continue, and many women *sarpanchs* have to face violence for challenging existing societal power centres. In other cases, women are in PRIs only in name.

In reality, it is the male family members who hold the power. In spite of the affirmative action in panchayati raj in favour of marginalized communities, exclusion of caste, poverty, tribal status, gender and caste sharply demarcate those who have political power from those who do not. Central and State Governments should not delay any further the devolution and decentralization of powers from higher bodies (Government of India or State Governments) to the panchayati raj structures. This devolution right now is lagging in almost all the States.

The three Fs—funds, functions and functionaries—in most States are still in the same position prior to 1993. In the absence of this basic requirement, the Constitutional provisions are not only being violated, but there is lack of clarity at the field level which leads to dysfunctional situations.

India has primarily relied upon the method of reservation to ensure women's presence in decision-making bodies. This has increased *de jure*, but not necessarily *de facto*, participation. There is need to encourage women's participation in other kinds of groups and associations which contribute to an atmosphere of leadership by women, as well as supporting training and networking for elected women.

New Delhi **Nupur Tiwari**

Abbreviations/Acronyms

3Fs	Functions, Funds, and Functionaries
AR&RS	Action Research and Research Studies
AV	Audio-Visual
BE	Budget Estimates
BRGF	Backward Regions Grant Fund
CB	Capacity Building
CB&T	Capacity Building and Training
CBT	Computer Based Tutorial
CSS	Centrally-sponsored Scheme
DI	Devolution Index
DPC	District Planning Committee
DPE	Decentralized Planning and Empowerment
ER	Elected Representative
EWR	Elected Women Representative
GoI	Government of India
GP	Gram Panchayat
GS	Gram Sabha
IAP	Integrated Action Plan
ICDS	Integrated Child Development Services
ICT	Information and Communication Technology
IEC	Information, Education, and Communication
IT	Information Technology
MDM	Mid-Day Meal
MFP	Minor Forest Produce
MGNREGA	The Mahatma Gandhi National Rural Employment Guarantee Act
MMP	Mission Mode Project
MoPR	Ministry of Panchayati Raj
NCBF	National Capacity Building Framework
NE	North East
NeGP	National e-Governance Plan
NIC	National Informatics Centre
NRHM	National Rural Health Mission

OBC	Other Backward Class
PB	Planning and Budget
PDS	Public Distribution System
PEAIS	Panchayat Empowerment and Accountability Incentive Scheme
PES	Panchayat Enterprise Suite
PESA	Panchayats (Extension to the Scheduled Areas) Act, 1996
PF	Panchayat Functionary
PMEYSA	Panchayat Mahila Evam Yuva Shakti Abhiyan
PMSA	Panchayat Mahila Shakti Abhiyan
PPP	Public-Private-Partnership
PR	Panchayati Raj
PRI	Panchayati Raj Institution
PRIA Soft	PRI Accounting System Software
RBH	Rural Business Hub
RD	Rural Development
RGGSP	Rashtriya Gaurav Gram Sabha Puraskar
RGPSA	Rajiv Gandhi Panchayat Sashaktikaran Abhiyan
RGSY	Rashtriya Gram Swaraj Yojana
RSVY	Rashtriya Sam Vikas Yojana
SCs	Scheduled Castes
SEC	State Election Commission
SFC	State Finance Commission
SIRD	State Institute of Rural Development
SSA	Sarva Shiksha Abhiyan
STs	Scheduled Tribes
TG&S	Technical Guidance and Support
TSI	Technical Support Institution
TSP	Tribal Sub Plan
UT	Union Territory

1

Local Self-governments in India

1.1 Constitutional Provisions Regarding Local Bodies

The Constitution of India has made detailed provisions for ensuring protection of democracy in Parliament and in State Legislatures. Hence, democracy in these institutions has survived and flourished. However, the Constitution did not make local self-government in urban areas a clear-cut Constitutional obligation. While Article 40 of the Constitution requires the strengthening of the units of local self-government in the States, particularly panchayati raj institutions, there is no specific reference to municipalities except implicitly in Entry 5 of List II (State List) in the Seventh Schedule of the Constitution, which places the subject of local self-government as a responsibility of the State. Entry 5 reads as under:

"Local government, that is to say, the constitution and powers of municipal corporations, improvement trusts, district boards, mining settlement authorities and other local authorities for the purpose of local self-government or village administration".

As a consequence of inadequate Constitutional provision for local self-government, democracy in municipal governance was not stable. Though the respective municipal acts of the States provided for regular elections to municipal bodies, they were frequently suspended and superseded for indefinite periods of time. Frequent and indefinite suspensions or supersessions eroded the very basis of local self-government and had a negative effect on democracy at the grassroots level. The general position with regard to financial resources of the municipal bodies was also not satisfactory. Over the years, there was a steady encroachment on the assigned functions and revenues of urban local bodies (ULBs) by specialized agencies of the State Governments.

In short, local bodies could not function effectively because of: (a) inadequate devolution of functions and financial powers, (b) failure to hold regular elections and prolonged supersession and (c) lack of participation from weaker sections of the society. Consequently, local bodies in many States had become weak and ineffective as units of self-government in the democratic set up of India.

The weakened status of ULBs crystallized public opinion in favour of a Constitutional guarantee to safeguard the interests of urban local bodies in order to provide for the following:

1. Regular and fair conduct of elections to these bodies.
2. Holding of elections within a specified time limit in case of supersession.
3. Adequate representation of SC/ST and women in the elected bodies.
4. Placing on firm footing the relationship between the State Governments and the urban local bodies with respect to: (a) functions and taxation powers of the urban local bodies and (b) arrangement for revenue sharing between the State Government and the urban local bodies.
5. Involvement of elected representatives at grassroots level in planning at the district and metropolitan levels.

1.2 Decentralisation Initiative, 1992

The Seventy-third and Seventy-fourth Amendment Bills relating to panchayats and municipalities respectively were introduced in the Parliament in September 1991 to provide constitutional remedy for the inadequacies plaguing these bodies which were unable to perform effectively as vibrant democratic units of self-government. The Bills were referred to two joint bodies of Parliament and after necessary revision were reintroduced in July 1992, and passed by the Parliament in December 1992. Both the Bills were ratified by the required number of States [Article 368(ii)] and the President gave his assent in April 1993. The Seventy-third Amendment Act relating to panchayats came into force from April 24, 1993. The Seventy-fourth Amendment Act relating to municipalities came into force from June 1, 1993. The changes made by the Seventy-third and Seventy-fourth Amendment Acts to the Constitution were of historical importance and are summarised in Table 1.1.

Table 1.1: Seventy-third and Seventy-fourth Constitutional Amendment Acts

Act	Date on which came into force	Amendments made
Constitution (Seventy-third Amendment) Act, 1992	24. 4. 1993	A new Part IX relating to panchayats was inserted. In clause (3) of Article 280, sub-clause (bb) was inserted which provides for measures to supplement the resources of the panchayats. Eleventh Schedule added to the Constitution which provides an illustrative list for the devolution of functions to panchayats.
Constitution (Seventy-fourth Amendment) Act, 1992	1. 6. 1993	A new Part IXA relating to municipalities was inserted. In clause (3) of Article 280, sub-clause (c) was re-lettered as sub-clause (d) and before sub-clause (d) as so re-lettered, sub-clause (c) was inserted which provides for measures to supplement the resources of the municipalities. Twelfth Schedule added to the Constitution which provides an illustrative list for the devolution of functions to municipalities.

Source: Government of India, Ministry of Law, Justice and Company Affairs, *Constitution of India.*

In short, panchayats and municipalities are now constitutional bodies forming third tier to the federal polity of India. India's decentralisation initiative in the form of Seventy-third and Seventy-fourth Amendments poses challenges and offers opportunities.

1.3 Constitution (Seventy-third Amendment) Act, 1992

The passage of the Constitution (Seventy-third Amendment) Act, 1992 marked a watershed in the history of modern India. With this amendment, a uniform structure of panchayats emerged throughout the country.

Article 243G read with Eleventh Schedule of the Constitution explicitly requires the States to devolve powers and authority on panchayats which may be necessary to enable them to function as institutions of self-government. The Eleventh Schedule of the Constitution is reproduced in Table 1.2.

Table 1.2: Eleventh Schedule of the Constitution (Article 243 G)

1.	Agriculture, including agricultural extension.
2.	Land improvement, implementation of land reforms, land consolidation and soil conservation.
3.	Minor irrigation, water management and watershed development.
4.	Animal husbandry, dairying and poultry.
5.	Fisheries.
6.	Social forestry and farm forestry.
7.	Minor forest produce.
8.	Small-scale industries, including food processing industries.
9.	Khadi, village and cottage industries.
10.	Rural housing.
11.	Drinking water
12.	Fuel and fodder.
13.	Roads, culverts, bridges, ferries, waterways and other means of communication.
14.	Rural electrification, including distribution of electricity.
15.	Non-conventional energy sources.

Contd...

16.	Poverty alleviation programmes.
17.	Education, including primary and secondary schools.
18.	Technical training and vocational education.
19.	Adult and non-formal education.
20.	Libraries.
21.	Cultural activities.
22.	Markets and fairs.
23.	Health and sanitation, including hospitals, primary health centres and dispensaries.
24.	Family welfare.
25.	Women and child development.
26.	Social welfare, including welfare of the handicapped and mentally retarded.
27.	Welfare of the weaker sections, and in particular, of the scheduled castes and the scheduled tribes.
28.	Public distribution system.
29.	Maintenance of community assets.

1.4 Constitution (Seventy-fourth Amendment) Act, 1992

The passage of the Constitution (Seventy-fourth Amendment) Act, 1992 was a landmark in the history of municipal administration in India. Article 243W read with Twelfth Schedule of the Constitution provides the illustrative list for the devolution of functions to the municipalities. The Twelfth Schedule of the Constitution is reproduced in Table 1.3. Many States have amended their municipal laws to ensure conformity with the new constitutional provisions.

Through this amendment, a new Part IX-A relating to municipalities was incorporated in the Constitution to provide for, *inter alia,* the constitution of three types of municipalities, viz. nagar panchayat for a transitional area, i.e. an area in transition from a rural to urban area [1]; Municipal Council for smaller urban area, and Municipal Corporation for larger urban area (Article 243Q).

The Constitution (Seventy-fourth Amendment) Act, 1992 conferred constitutional status to the structure and mandate of municipalities so as to enable them to function as vibrant democratic and self-governing institutions at the grassroots level.

Table 1.3: Twelfth Schedule of the Constitution (Article 243W)

1.	Urban planning including town planning.
2.	Regulation of land-use and construction of buildings.
3.	Planning for economic and social development.
4.	Roads and bridges.
5.	Water supply for domestic, industrial and commercial purposes.
6.	Public health, sanitation conservancy and solid waste management.
7.	Fire services.
8.	Urban forestry, protection of the environment and promotion of ecological aspects.
9.	Safeguarding the interests of weaker sections of society, including the handicapped and mentally retarded.
10.	Slum improvement and upgradation.
11.	Urban poverty alleviation.
12.	Provision of urban amenities and facilities such as parks, gardens, play-grounds.
13.	Promotion of cultural, educational and aesthetic aspects.
14.	Burials and burial grounds; cremations, cremation grounds and electric crematoriums.
15.	Cattle ponds; prevention of cruelty to animals.
16.	Vital statistics including registration of births and deaths.
17.	Public amenities including street lighting, parking lots, bus stops and public conveniences.
18.	Regulation of slaughter houses and tanneries.

The objectives of the Seventy-fourth Amendment included decentralisation of power and popular participation in the planning, management, and delivery of civic services.

1.5 Women in Local Governance Structures

Legislative enactments have dramatically increased women's access to decision-making structures in recent years. The Seventy-third and Seventy-fourth Constitutional

Amendments passed in 1993 provided for reservation of 33 percent of elected seats for women at different levels of local governance in both rural and urban local bodies. Also there would be one-third reservation for women to posts of chairperson of these bodies. One-third of the seats were further reserved for women belonging to the SC/ST community. The Panchayats (Extension to Schedule Areas) Act, 1996 (PESA) made this amendment applicable to Schedule V areas. This has dramatically increased women's participation in local bodies. For every 5 year tenure of local governments, about 1 million women get elected to panchayats and local bodies. In some states, the number of elected women exceeds the reserved one-third quota.

The Constitution provides for rotation of seats reserved for women but does not prescribe the number of terms for which seats may be served for rotation. Seats are reserved for one term, two terms or more depending upon the provisions made by the State Legislature in the State law. The option to reserve seats for more than one terms is open, but it is for the State Legislature to decide the number of terms for which seats will remain reserved. Tamil Nadu has taken a positive step by freezing the reserved seats for women for two terms.

Local government institutions have not been given full financial and political powers to function independently but 29 subjects ranging from agriculture to poverty eradication have been devolved to these institutions. In theory, the presidents of the gram panchayats, block panchayats and district panchayats are responsible for prioritising the developmental needs of the villagers and allocating the grants accordingly. In practice, the level of responsiveness and manner of functioning of the panchayats varies considerably across states. As far as women's participation is concerned, the legislative enactments have ensured that they are represented in all states.

Many of the elected women entering the public arena for the first time lack confidence, feel isolated, and have no previous political experience. They need to develop their innate leadership skills. Studies conducted in different parts of the country show that 95 percent of the elected women representatives (EWRs) are first-timers in politics and join politics because that is what their male family/village members want. As first timers without previous exposure to politics, many of the elected women lack the capacity to function properly in the panchayats and municipalities, and consequently are not taken seriously by their colleagues. Sustained training and networking efforts are being undertaken both by government and non-government agencies to ensure that women's capacity to participate improves. With just a few years of experience, women have emerged as articulate, motivated leaders all over the country.

Gender budgeting involving grassroots elected women representatives is being used for advocacy in several places. Increased networking and formation of confederations of elected women representatives has helped to strengthen women's leadership. This approach has been especially successful in southern and western India. The formation of these networks promotes solidarity among the elected women representatives, otherwise divided by caste, religion and geographical boundaries. Thus, formation of these networks is the first step in the direction of empowering women. Their position as panchayat members adds to their ability to intervene and negotiate with the community. The presence of EWRs in the dispute resolution process lends support and confidence to other women. The networks have also been able to promote capacity building.

1.5.1 Proxy Politics: Constitutional provisions apart, there are complaints from various parts of the country regarding effective participation of women in local governance structures. Proxy politics, power brokering and gender discrimination continue, and many women *sarpanchs* have to face violence for challenging existing societal power centres. In other cases, women are in PRI only in name. In reality, it is the male family members who hold the power. In spite of the affirmative action in panchayati raj in favour of marginalized communities, exclusion of caste, poverty, tribal status, gender and caste sharply demarcate those who have political power from those who do not. Central and State Governments should not delay any further the devolution and decentralization of powers from higher bodies (Government of India or State Governments) to the panchayati raj structures. This devolution right now is lagging in almost all the States. The three Fs—funds, functions and functionaries—in most States are still in the same position prior to 1993. In the absence of this basic requirement, the Constitutional provisions are not only being violated, but there is lack of clarity at the field level which leads to dysfunctional situations.

India has primarily relied upon the method of reservation to ensure women's presence in decision-making bodies. This has increased *de jure*, but not necessarily *de facto*, participation. There is need to encourage women's participation in other kinds of groups and associations which contribute to an atmosphere of leadership by women, as well as supporting training and networking for elected women.

1.5.2 Amendment to Article 243T of the Constitution to Provide for 50 percent Reservation for Women in Urban Local Bodies: The Constitution (112th Amendment) Bill, 2009 to provide for 50 percent reservation of women in Urban Local Bodies was introduced in Lok Sabha on November 24, 2009. Through this Bill, the Government of India seeks to increase the representation of women in urban local bodies (ULBs) from the present level of one-third to 50 percent which would also include enhancement of reservation for women upto 50 percent in seats reserved for scheduled castes, scheduled tribes, and 50 percent reservations for women in the posts of chairpersons. This would result in increased representation of women in ULBs and is likely to yield significant benefits in terms of higher priority to women's issues in critical areas of urban governance and service delivery such as water supply, sanitation, solid waste management, education and health, etc. The bill is under the consideration of the Parliamentary Standing Committee on Urban Development.

Endnote

1. Here, 'a transitional area', 'a smaller urban area', or 'a larger urban area' means such area as the Governor may specify by public notification having regard to the population of the area, the density of the population, the revenue generated for local administration, the percentage of employment in non-agricultural activities and such other factors.

2

Constitutional and Legal Provisions Regarding Panchayati Raj Institutions (PRIs)

The need and demand for good governance has increased with the rapid expansion of the economy and the growing awareness and assertion of rights by an increasingly educated population. Accountable, participatory and good governance is critical for ensuring social inclusion. The significant rise in expenditure on programmes for social inclusion in recent years needs to be matched with improved implementation for enhanced impact at the local level. The role of Panchayats, the constitutionally mandated local self-governments at the grassroots level, is critical in this context.

2.1 Constitutional Provisions Regarding Panchayats

Panchayats are local governments mandated in the Constitution of India. As per the Constitution, a three-tier structure of Panchayats is in place across the country, excepting areas where Part IX of the Constitution does not apply. Panchayats are to be constituted, through elections every five years, except in States with population less than 20 lakh, where panchayats at two tiers may be created.

As in 2014-2015, there were 2.51 lakh Panchayats and 29.16 lakh elected representatives (ERs). The Constitution leaves it to the discretion of the States to devolve funds, functions and functionaries (3Fs) to the panchayats and States vary a great deal in the extent to which they have devolved powers to panchayats and equipped them with adequate manpower, infrastructure including office space and furniture, modern equipment, training etc., to enable them to perform their functions. An illustrative list of functions which can be devolved on the PRIs is given in Schedule XI of the Constitution.

The Constitution recognizes the gram sabha, i.e. all the electors in a village panchayat. The Constitution provides that seats and offices of chairpersons be reserved for the scheduled castes (SCs) and scheduled tribes (STs) in proportion to their respective population, and not less than one-third seats and offices of chairpersons be reserved for women, including within SCs and STs reservations.

Article 243 ZD of the Constitution mandates the setting up of district planning committees (DPCs) in every district, to consolidate the plans prepared by the panchayats and municipalities in the district and to prepare the draft development plan for the entire district.

The Constitution provides that State Election Commissions (SECs) be set up and vested with the superintendence, direction and control of the preparation of electoral rolls and the conduct of elections to the panchayats. The Constitution further provides that State Finance Commissions (SFCs) be constituted every five years. SFCs are to make recommendations to the Governor regarding the distribution between the State and panchayats of the net proceeds of taxes, duties, toll, fees etc., the determination of taxes, duties, tolls and fees which may be assigned to, or appropriated by the panchayats, and grants-in-aid to the panchayats from the Consolidated Fund of the State, as well as measures needed to improve the financial position of panchayats.

2.2 Panchayats (Extension to Scheduled Areas) Act, 1996 (PESA)

Article 243M of the Constitution, while exempting the Fifth Schedule areas from Part IX of the Constitution, provides that the Parliament may by law extend its provisions to the scheduled and tribal areas subject to such exceptions and modifications as may be specified in such law and no such law shall be deemed to be an amendment to the Constitution. On the basis of the report of the Bhuria Committee submitted in 1995, the Parliament enacted the Panchayats (Extension to Scheduled Areas) Act, 1996 (PESA) to extend Part IX of the

Constitution with certain modifications and exceptions to the Scheduled V areas of 9 States.

PESA envisages self-governance through the gram sabha, and, while extending the panchayati raj structure as envisaged in Part IX of the Constitution, gives wide powers to the gram sabhas in Schedule V areas.

PESA lays a framework of self-governance and people's control over resources through the gram sabhas in Schedule V areas. Yet, the implementation of PESA has not been satisfactory, partly because of the lack of interest shown by States to amend State laws in compliance with PESA provisions, but also because of the inadequacy of efforts to strengthen gram sabhas. Strengthening of panchayats and implementation of PESA in Schedule V areas has significant national importance as it can lead to improved governance and accountability in these areas. See also section 3.8 of chapter 3 of this book.

2.3 Areas Not Covered under Part IX

While Part IX of the Constitution applies to a vast majority of the country, as per Article 243M of the Constitution, some areas are exempted from Part IX. These include the States of Meghalaya, Mizoram and Nagaland, areas covered under the Sixth Schedule, the hill areas of Manipur and the district level panchayats in the hill areas of Darjeeling. Various kinds of grassroots local governance structures exist in these areas.

Following a decision of Committee of Secretaries in April 2010, the Ministry of Panchayati Raj (MoPR), with the participation of Ministry of Home Affairs, Ministry of DoNER, Ministry of Tribal Affairs and Ministry of Urban Development has been taking up the cause of decentralized democratic governance in the North-East (NE) in consultation with State Governments from 2011. It is necessary to follow this up with technical and financial support for democratic decentralization through elections, women's representation, accountability to the gram sabha, and devolution of functions in these areas.

2.4 Role of the States

Within the above broad framework, as local government is a State subject, State legislatures have a critical role in determining various aspects of panchayati raj in their States. States are key as far as devolution of powers to panchayats is concerned. The Constitution envisages that panchayats will function as institutions of local government and prepare plans and implement schemes for economic development and social justice, but leaves the precise devolution of powers and authority to panchayats to the States. The State legislatures are to consider the 29 matters illustratively set out in the Eleventh Schedule of the Constitution for devolution to the panchayats for the planning and implementation of schemes for economic development and social justice. Powers to impose taxes by and provision of funds to the panchayats are determined by the State. The powers of gram sabhas are also decided by States. Moreover, States play a critical role in building panchayat capacities and in creating an appropriate framework for accountability and transparency.

Traditionally, Centrally-sponsored Schemes (CSSs) and additional central assistance (ACAs) have been developed along the jurisdictional lines of the Ministries and Departments, based on vertical management decision systems. In such vertical implementation structures, it is difficult to ensure that context-specific measures to address the issues at hand in a holistic manner are taken up. Only through panchayats, which are constitutionally mandated local democratic institutions, can people's participation and accountability to people be ensured. A strong panchayati raj system is critical for good governance.

An important concern that is often raised by Central Ministries and State Governments regarding devolving more programmes and activities to panchayats is that panchayats have poor capacity and will not be able to deliver. And in fact, the weakness in terms of administrative and technical capacity within panchayats is an area of concern. This leads to a vicious cycle, i.e. low capacity, leading to inadequate devolution, and leading to disempowered institutions. It is, therefore, essential to build the capacity of panchayats and related institutions. In particular, gram sabha processes have to be supported for the sake of creating awareness about the opportunities and programmes of the Government available for their development, transparency, accountability and efficient delivery of services.

Developing a strong panchayati raj system, essential to improve governance and delivery of services, involves redistribution of power, institution building and development of processes that improve accountability to the people. It requires planned and strategic interventions tied to specified deliverables on the part of States to enable them to stay committed to strengthening panchayats and elected local bodies.

3

Ministry of Panchayati Raj (MoPR) and its Programmes/Schemes

3.1 Ministry of Panchayati Raj (MoPR)

The Ministry of Panchayati Raj was created as a separate Ministry on 27th May, 2004. It has the primary objective of implementation of Part IX of the Constitution, panchayats in Fifth Schedule Areas and district planning committees (as per Article 243ZD), and PESA. Since under the scheme of things in the Constitution, most of the actions including framing of laws rests with the State Government, the Ministry strives to reach its goals primarily through advocacy, and also through financial support.

- **Vision:** To attain decentralised and participatory local self-government through panchayati raj institutions (PRIs).
- **Mission:** Empowerment, enablement and accountability of PRIs to ensure inclusive development with social justice, and efficient delivery of services.

The Ministry works to fulfil its mandate in various ways. Firstly, through its schemes, it promotes and provides funds for key activities. Secondly, it plays a strong advocacy role. MoPR fosters knowledge creation and sharing so that the issues to be addressed are clearly articulated, meaningful strategies formulated, and there is sharing within government as well as with non-government agencies and experts.

3.2 Number of Panchayats and Elected Representatives

There are 2.51 lakh panchayats in the country, which include 2.39 lakh gram panchayats, 6,405 block panchayats and 589 district panchayats, or zilla parishads. The position of elected representatives is given in Table 3.1.

Table 3.1: Panchayats and Elected Representatives

S. No.	Panchayat	Total number of elected representatives (lakh)	Percent of elected women	Percent of elected SCs	Percent of elected STs
1.	Gram Panchayat	27.32	43.81	22.99	10.01
2.	Block Panchayat	1.68	40.03	19.39	7.07
3.	Zilla Panchayat	0.16	43.19	16.57	10.78
	Total	**29.16**			

Source: Government of India, Ministry of Panchayati Raj, *Annual Report, 2014-15*, p. 2.

MoPR has been implementing various schemes to strengthen panchayati raj in the country, by building panchayat capacities on the one hand, and encouraging and supporting States to devolve powers to panchayats and take measures to promote transparency and accountability, on the other hand.

It provides financial support to academic institutions, NGOs, research organizations etc. to undertake research to provide an in-depth analysis of long-term issues, impacts and experiences in panchayati raj across the country.

3.3 Devolution of Powers, Responsibilities and Resources to Panchayats

Panchayat is a State subject and as per the Constitution, the devolution of powers and authority to panchayats has been left to the discretion of States. As per Article 243G of the Constitution, the State Legislatures are to consider the 29 matters illustratively set out in the Eleventh Schedule for devolution to the panchayats.

The devolution of powers, responsibilities and resources to panchayats is considered essential for sustainable decentralization and inclusive development. MoPR continuously advocates with and persuades State Governments to devolve powers to

Panchayats.

3.3.1 Activity Mapping of Functions Devolved by States to Panchayats: For effective devolution, there should be a clear cut delineation of functions for each level of the local government. Clarity on the role and responsibilities of the panchayats of different tiers is provided by 'activity mapping', which becomes an important step in the devolution of functions to the panchayats.

Activity mapping means, the unbundling of subjects or sectors and assignment of various activities to different levels of government on the basis of clear principles of public finance and public accountability, and above all, the governance principles of subsidiarity, democratic decentralization and citizen centricity.

The result of good activity mapping would be to clearly identify where competence, authority and accountability lie. MoPR has supported States in preparing activity maps to delineate the roadmap for devolution.

3.3.2 Schematic Interventions: MoPR has redoubled its efforts since 2012-13 to promote devolution of powers from States to panchayats by linking 20 percent funds of the Rajiv Gandhi Panchayat Sashaktikaran Abhiyan (RGPSA) to performance on various indicators that set an appropriate policy framework for panchayats, which include devolution. While submitting the annual plan proposals under RGPSA, States have to submit before the central executive committee (CEC) of RGPSA, the status of devolution of 3Fs (funds, functions and functionaries), and initiatives taken by them. The performance of States on this count is also assessed.

3.3.3 Panchayat Devolution Index: To encourage States to empower panchayats, the performance of States regarding devolution is measured through a panchayat devolution index (PDI) every year. The PDI is prepared by an independent agency and awards are given to the States which rank high on PDI.

MoPR has continuously refined the scope and

methodology of the PDI. Since 2008-09, evaluation of States has been based on a two-stage assessment. In the first stage, States are assessed on the fulfilment of the following fundamental Constitutional requirements:

1. Establishment of state election commission.
2. Holding of elections to the PRIs.
3. Setting up of state finance commission.
4. Constitution of the district planning committees.
5. Reservation of seats for SCs/STs and women (effective from 2013-14).

States that fulfil each of these fundamental requirements, qualify for evaluation in terms of various indicators of the PDI. The indicators of the PDI aim at assessing the state of devolution in respect of the funds, functions, and functionaries by the States to the PRIs. The studies from 2010-11 to 2013-14 have assessed the States on cumulative as well as incremental PDI. The cumulative PDI measures the performance of States till date. States that have historically had strong panchayati raj systems tend to rank high on the cumulative PDI.

The incremental PDI, measures the performance of States over one year. With the introduction of the incremental PDI, States that do not have strong panchayati raj systems historically, but have taken important measures during the year, can also win prizes. This has generated a new enthusiasm among States.

3.3.4 Delegation of Powers in Centrally-sponsored Schemes to Panchayats: MoPR advocates a strong role for Panchayats in Centrally-sponsored Schemes (CSSs) that aim at the social-economic development of the rural people, so that these schemes can become more context specific and a greater measure of accountability and transparency can be introduced. At present, there is a great deal of variation across CSSs in the extent to which the role for panchayats is envisaged. While schemes such as the Mahatma Gandhi National Rural Employment Guarantee Act, the Sakshar Bharat Abhiyan, National Rural Drinking Water Programme etc. provide a substantial role for Panchayats, in several CSSs, the role of panchayats has not been articulated, and various grassroots parallel bodies have been set up instead.

MoPR, therefore, constituted an Expert Committee under the chairpersonship of Shri Mani Shankar Aiyar, in 2012, to: (i) review the existing policy and guidelines of relevant Central Sector/Centrally-sponsored Schemes dealing with social sector and anti-poverty programmes and to give specific recommendations. recommendations on: (a) appropriate role and responsibility of panchayats at different levels based on the principle of subsidiarity, (b) strengthening their capacity to deliver services and (c) making them accountable to respective gram sabhas; (ii) the constraints that may come up in operationalizing the delivery system through the PRIs and suggest ways and means of dealing with the same; and (iii) ways to incentivize States to devolve 3Fs to panchayats.

The Committee submitted its report in April 2013. The report contains several recommendations for empowerment of PRIs, which include revision of CSS guidelines and activity mapping for CSSs for providing role and responsibilities to the PRIs. The Expert Committee has also given model activity mapping for the schemes administered by eight Ministries and Departments, namely Rural Development, Agriculture and Cooperation, Water Resources, Rural Drinking Water and Sanitation, School Education and Literacy, Health and Family Welfare, Women and Child Development and Tribal Affairs.

The report of the Expert Committee was circulated to all the State Governments and Central Ministries for taking action.

3.4 Backward Regions Grant Fund (BRGF) Programme

3.4.1 Introduction: To address the issues of regional imbalances in development processes, (BRGF) Programme was launched on February 19, 2007. The BRGF Programme (District component), administered by MoPR, now covers 272 backward districts in 28 States.

With its emphasis on participative plans prepared from the

grassroots level upwards rather than the top down approach, the BRGF Programme represents a major shift in approach towards planning. The guidelines of the Programme stipulate the central role in planning and implementation of the Programme for panchayats in rural areas and municipalities in urban areas. The conviction that drives BRGF's locally-driven approach is that grassroots level democratic institutions know best about the dimensions of socio-economic development issues, particularly felt needs/necessities in their areas and are, therefore, best placed to undertake individually small, but overall significant local interventions to sustainably tackle local developmental issues, including deprivation. A key feature under BRGF is that, in the interests of clarity and consistency, each State is to indicate the normative formula to be used for the allocation of BRGF funds to each tier of panchayat and ULB in the district.

3.4.2 Management of the Programme at the State Government Level: Each State Government has designated a department, in most cases, the Department of Panchayati Raj, as the nodal department at the State level, to be responsible for the management, monitoring and evaluation of the Programme. A high-powered committee (HPC) headed by the state chief secretary and including, *inter alia*, the development commissioner, state secretaries of departments of planning, panchayati raj, urban development, and other sectors under which works are going to be taken up under the Programme, approves the capacity building plan. A representative of the Ministry of Panchayati Raj, the state plan adviser of the NITI Aayog and other Government of India nominees as deemed necessary are also included to review the implementation of the Programme.

Besides approving the capacity building plans, HPC is also required to review: (a) the formula governing the distribution of BRGF funds among the various tiers of panchayats and municipalities, (b) the formula for distribution of BRGF funds meant for welfare of SC/ST and (c) the system of accountability and monitoring of the works.

3.4.3 Special Provisions for States and Districts not covered under Parts IX & IX-A of the Constitution: Special provisions have been made in the BRGF guidelines for the districts/areas in the States of J&K, Assam, Manipur, Meghalaya, Mizoram, Nagaland and Tripura which do not have panchayats. The village level bodies and institutions in these districts constituted under local laws or executive instructions are empowered to plan and implement the programme in these areas.

3.4.4 Fund Flow Mechanism and Tracking of Funds under the BRGF: All funds sanctioned by the Ministry under the Programme are transferred directly to the Consolidated Fund of the State Government concerned. These funds are required to be transferred to the implementing entities, i.e. panchayats, municipalities etc. by the State Government within 15 days, failing which the States are required to pay penal interest at RBI rate.

3.4.5 BRGF Development Grants: BRGF is a highly process-oriented programme and the quality of its implementation depends upon the institutional strength of panchayats and municipalities and district planning machinery in a State. The quality of district plans, on which BRGF proposals are based, vary from State to State. District plans received from the various States indicate that the untied fund allocated to the districts are generally being used for filling infrastructural gaps in works relating to drinking water, connectivity, health, education, social sectors, electrification etc.

3.4.6 BRGF Capacity Building Grants: MoPR's National Capacity Building Framework 2014 (NCBF-2014) envisages strengthening of institutional arrangements, including the infrastructure, as well as extending software support for capacity building of elected representatives, government functionaries and other stakeholders of panchayats and municipalities. In pursuance of the NCBF-2014, each State is required to identify nodal authorities for preparation and implementation of a six-year perspective capacity building plan and annual capacity building plan.

3.4.7 Constitution of District Planning Fund Committees (DPCs): One of the mandatory conditions for release of the development grant under BRGF is that the district plans prepared by local bodies need to be consolidated by the district planning committees. This provision has strengthened and activated DPCs across the country. When BRGF was launched in 2007, of the 24 States to which Part IX and IX-A of the Constitution was applicable, only 13 States had duly constituted the DPCs. As a result of the BRGF Programme, all the BRGF States have now constituted DPCs or equivalent bodies for the concerned districts.

3.4.8 Technical Support for DPCs to Prepare District Plans: The Ministry has empanelled certain institutions having expertise in technical and developmental issues as technical support institutions (TSIs) to help the preparation of district perspective plans and annual district plans. The Ministry has provided detailed timelines for the various steps to be followed in preparing such plans. The Ministry has also provided the draft memorandum of understanding (MoU) to be signed by the State Government, district planning committee and the TSI. The TSIs are also required to capture the participatory planning process in the PlanPlus software—one of the 10 software applications rolled out under the e-Panchayat Mission Mode Project.

3.4.9 PlanPlus Software Application: The current planning system largely involves preparation of scheme-wise plans at the district level often resulting in lack of convergence with other schematic/sectoral funds. To address these concerns, the Ministry of Panchayati Raj has conceived a software viz. PlanPlus, one of the software applications under the e-Panchayat Mission Mode Project (MMP) which is made available to the rural and urban local bodies (RLBs and ULBs) and line departments for preparing inclusive and participative decentralized plans. The Application facilitates the consolidation and integration of the plans of all planning units in the district (including urban and rural local bodies and line departments) to generate a comprehensive and consolidated district plan. Citizens can also view the activities being planned in their respective areas. It also encourages participation among planning units by facilitating one planning unit to make suggestions to another planning unit. The Ministry has been continuously promoting decentralized planning at the grassroots level through the PlanPlus Application. Currently, generation of plans through PlanPlus has been prescribed as one of the necessary requirement for the release of BRGF funds.

3.4.10 Action Soft: ActionSoft is another important PES Application which works in collaboration with PlanPlus and captures the work execution flow, facilitates decentralized reporting of progress of work execution, converges and keeps track of the flow of funds from different sources during implementation, converges the rural and urban plan units to report the physical and financial progress of works and brings about total transparency in the reporting of physical and financial progress. To assist the application on the similar lines, mActionSoft, which is a mobile application, is being developed.

3.5 Capacity Building and Training (CB&T)

CB&T of various stakeholders of panchayats is a complex task, as it involves large numbers—there are 29.16 lakh elected representatives (ERs) alone—as well as a range of stakeholders. These include ERs, panchayat functionaries including panchayat development officers, secretaries, accountants, water pump operators, gram sabhas or citizens, experts, and media persons. The challenge is to reach out to this diverse group while ensuring high quality, context-specific CB&T. Moreover, as panchayats are local governments, the subjects to be covered are also large: ranging from management, finance, social mobilization to the 29 subject areas that are to be developed in panchayats.

3.5.1 Initiatives for Capacity Building: MoPR has supported the CB&T of panchayat ERs and functionaries, as well as other stakeholders in several ways. Under RGPSA as well as the CB grant of BRGF, substantial support has been provided to set up the training infrastructure, and to provide training. In addition, MoPR arranges sharing across States and also supports knowledge based activities.

MoPR, along with States, has successfully addressed the challenge of large numbers for training by deploying the cascade mode of training as well as distance education. Around 15 lakh panchayat elected representatives and functionaries are trained every year. Several training institutes have also innovated with interesting modes of training, such as on-the-spot training, workbooks, help desks, street plays etc. Exposure visits of elected representatives to well-performing panchayats have also been organized. The range of stakeholders to be trained has also expanded considerably, to include various technical functionaries, gram sabhas, school children etc. Very strong efforts have been undertaken under RGPSA to strengthen the institutional structure for training.

3.5.2 National Capability Building Framework (NCBF): NCBF for the capability building of panchayats was first prepared in 2006 by the MoPR, and laid out the broad principles, areas and methodologies for the capacity building of panchayats. Subsequently, many government and non-government training institutes undertook training of panchayat representatives and functionaries. They encountered many problems and innovated in various ways.

Consequently, MoPR decided to revise the NCBF on the basis of the lessons learnt so far. With intensive involvement of State Institutes of Rural Development (SIRDs) as well as non-government resource institutions, the best practices followed in capacity building of panchayats across the country were documented. These were discussed in regional and national workshops, in which recommendations were made in the following areas:

1. Expanding outreach of training.
2. Modes of training.
3. Areas of training.
4. Quality of training.
5. Training of SCs, STs and women representatives.
6. Institutional structures and processes.

3.6 Rajiv Gandhi Panchayat Sashaktikaran Abhiyan (RGPSA)

See chapter 4 of this book.

3.7 E-Panchayat

As per the World Bank, "E-government refers to the use by government agencies of information technologies (such as wide area networks, the internet, and mobile computing) that have the ability to transform relations with citizens, businesses, and other arms of government". Government of India, with an intention to transform the governance landscape by ensuring participation of citizens in policy making and providing ease of access to information to the citizens, introduced the National e-Governance Plan (NeGP) in 2006. The vision of the NeGP was to "make all Government services accessible to the common man in his locality, through common service delivery outlets and ensure efficiency, transparency and reliability of such services at affordable costs to realise the basic needs of the common man".

E-panchayat is one of the Mission Mode Project (MMP), currently being implemented with a vision to empower and transform rural India.

As a first step towards formulating the project, the Ministry of Panchayati Raj constituted an Expert Group in June, 2007 under the Chairmanship of Dr. B.K. Gairola, Director General, NIC, Government of India. The Expert Group was entrusted with the task of assessing the IT programmes of Ministry of Panchayati Raj and recommending cost effective solutions along with the cost implications.

Adopting a consultative approach, the Committee interacted with the States/UTs to assess the existing status of computerization up to the gram panchayat level, including the initiatives undertaken by the State Governments.

In order to understand the ground realities, the Committee conducted field visits to some of the gram panchayats in the selected rural areas where some IT initiatives had been undertaken. Inputs from eminent experts in the public and private sector were also taken into account as part of the consultative process. In essence, it found that while some computerization efforts had already been made at panchayat level by States like Gujarat, West Bengal, Karnataka, Kerala, Andhra Pradesh and Goa, these attempts were limited as they were driven by short-term goals and were unable to completely transform panchayats due to lack of a holistic perspective. It was felt that a more comprehensive approach was required to make a cognizable impact on the functioning of the panchayats for the benefit of the citizens. These recommendations formed the basis for the conceptualization of E-panchayat MMP.

The E-panchayat project holds great promise for the rural masses as it aims to transform the panchayati raj institutions (PRIs) into symbols of modernity, transparency and efficiency. This is a one of its kind nationwide IT initiative introduced by Ministry of Panchayati Raj that endeavours to ensure people's participation in programme decision-making, implementation and delivery. The project aims to automate the functioning of the 2.5 lakh panchayats in the country. The project addresses all aspects of panchayats' functioning including planning, monitoring, implementation, budgeting, accounting, social audit and delivery of citizen services like issue of certificates, licenses etc.

Subsequently, E-panchayat scheme was subsumed by Rajiv Gandhi Panchayat Sashaktikaran Abhiyan (RGPSA).

3.8 Panchayats Extension to Scheduled Areas Act, 1996 (PESA)

3.8.1 Scope: A major function of the MoPR is to oversee

the implementation of the provisions of PESA, by the 10 States that have areas listed in the Fifth Schedule, namely Andhra Pradesh, Chhattisgarh, Gujarat, Himachal Pradesh, Jharkhand, Madhya Pradesh, Maharashtra, Odisha, Rajasthan and Telangana. There are 108 districts in the 10 states as mentioned above, out of which 45 are fully and 63 are partially notified under the Fifth Schedule of the Constitution.

3.8.2 Powers of Gram Sabha: PESA provides wide powers to the gram sabhas. The gram sabhas under PESA are deemed to be competent to safeguard and preserve the traditions of their people, community resources and customary mode of dispute resolution. The gram sabhas further have:

1. Mandatory executive functions to approve plans of the village panchayats, identify beneficiaries for schemes, issue certificates of utilization of funds.
2. Right to mandatory consultation in matters of land acquisition, resettlement and rehabilitation, and prospecting licenses/mining leases for minor minerals.
3. Power to prevent alienation of land and restore alienated land.
4. Power to regulate and restrict sale/consumption of liquor.
5. Power to manage village markets and control money lending to STs.
6. Ownership of minor forest produce.
7. Power to control institutions and functionaries in all social sectors.
8. Power to control local plans and resources for such plans including TSP etc.

3.8.3 Challenges: In spite of the critical importance of implementing PESA in the Fifth Schedule areas, there are many operational issues acting as constraints in the implementation of PESA. Some State and Central subject laws relating to mines and minerals, forests, land acquisition etc. are yet to be made PESA compliant. 5 out of 10 States are yet to frame appropriate rules under PESA, resulting in delays in implementation of the PESA in letter and spirit. The functioning of gram sabhas has to be made effective by ensuring participation of government functionaries in the meetings of gram sabhas. Capacities of gram sabhas as well as elected representatives have to be built. This will help in channelizing the generation of demands by the villagers and also in the accountability of the functionaries, particularly in the left wing extremism affected areas. There is a need to monitor the implementation of the Act at the district and State levels.

3.8.4 MoPR Initiatives: Strengthening the gram sabha, capacity building and training of elected representatives in these areas and ensuring compliance of State Panchayati Raj Acts and subject laws to PESA provisions remain the focus of the Ministry's activity. Guidelines on implementation of PESA have been issued to all Fifth Schedule States by the Ministry. MoPR has urged the State Governments to take the following steps to ensure implementation of PESA Act:

A. Functioning of Gram Sabha:

- Constitute gram sabha as per PESA Act.
- Empower gram sabha and ensure effective functioning.
- Regular training of Government and panchayat functionaries on PESA.

B. Empower Gram Panchayats:

- Provide manpower, infrastructure and build capacities.
- Devolve 3Fs including control over local institutions and functionaries.
- Involve government officials in functioning and empowerment of panchayats.

C. Administrative Measures:

- Committee of relevant departments and experts at State and District levels to review and ensure PESA compliance.
- Activate tribal advisory councils and tribal research institutes.
- Include implementation of PESA in Governor's annual report.
- Build capacity of elected representatives of PRIs.

- Sensitise government officers at various levels on issues related to PESA.

3.9 Panchayat Awards

The Ministry of Panchayati Raj (MoPR) incentivizes best performing panchayats and gram sabhas, and also documents their best practices. The incentivisation of best performing panchayats and gram sabhas is important for several reasons. Firstly, it encourages panchayat representatives who make special efforts. Secondly, it creates models for the panchayats and gram sabhas to follow. Thirdly, it focuses public attention on panchayat performance, which encourages all panchayats to improve their performance. Finally, this creates an ecosystem for overall good governance at the local level.

3.9.1 Panchayat Sashaktikaran Puraskar: Since 2011-12, panchayats have been incentivized for their performance under the modified Panchayat Empowerment and Accountability Incentive Scheme (PEAIS), now subsumed in Rajiv Gandhi Panchayat Sashaktikaran Abhiyan (RGPSA). Under the modified scheme, model indicators, questionnaires and marking scheme have been developed by the Ministry. Subsequently, the States/UTs adopted the indicators, questionnaire and marking scheme in their context.

The best performing panchayats have been incentivized on the basis of their performance on the following six aspects:

- **Panchayat Functioning:** (a) panchayat functioning, (b) functioning of gram sabhas, and (c) functioning of standing committee.
- **Management of Officials:** (a) training, (b) attendance of officials in panchayat meetings and (c) review.
- **Planning and Budget Formulation:** (a) preparation of annual plan, (b) process of preparation of annual plan and (c) budget.
- **Income Generation:** (a) planning for own income, (b) collection of dues and (c) voluntary contributions.
- **Performance:** (a) physical achievements, (b) expenditure

against budget in scheme, (c) expenditure on SCs/STs, (d) expenditure on women, (e) untied funds expenditure, (f) performance of civic duties, panchayat and local institutions, (g) panchayat and community groups, (h) special initiatives and (i) IEC initiatives

- **Accountability and Transparency:** (a) maintenance of accounts, (b) audit, (c) grievance redressal and (d) compliance to RTI.

The best performing panchayats are identified on the basis of information provided by the panchayats on a circulated questionnaire, and field verification at the State level as well as the National level. Since 2011-12, the MoPR has been publishing a document on best practices followed by the award winning best performing panchayats. The document is also made available on the Ministry's website for wider dissemination. The documentation of best practices has thrown up a range of areas in which panchayats have innovated. These have included, *inter alia*, the following:

- Innovative ways of revenue generation.
- Social mobilization.
- Support to self-help groups, farmers' groups, fishermen's groups etc.
- Enhancing livelihoods.
- Support to schools.
- Initiatives to address malnutrition.
- Child sex ratio and promoting children's health.
- Programmes for the aged and disabled.
- Water conservation and infrastructure creation.
- Empowerment of women.

An assessment of the award process has shown a high impact of this intervention, and that neighbouring panchayats visit these best performing panchayats and try to learn from them. Further, the performance framework developed has also been used by some State Governments to identify poorly performing panchayats (known as 'on watch' panchayats), by several States and provide them with special support.

3.9.2 Rashtriya Gaurav Gram Sabha (RGGS) Award: RGGS Puraskar was instituted by MoPR in 2010 to appreciate and encourage gram panchayats for making gram sabhas effective. The objective of instituting this award is to strengthen the institution of gram sabha and to highlight it as the institution for decision-making and social audit.

For selection of best performing panchayats under the RGGS award, parameters have been laid down by MoPR. These include the frequency with which gram sabhas are conducted, level of participation in the gram sabhas including the participation of marginalized groups, attendance of officials, issues discussed in the gram sabha and positive outcome achieved, status of social audit and transparency, convening of ward sabha and mahila sabha prior to gram sabha meetings, and maintenance of records.

State and district level committees have been formed to undertake the selection. Nominations are invited from gram panchayats. The information provided by the gram panchayats is scrutinized by district and state level committees and subsequently by a committee set up by MoPR, and the list of awardees is finalized. Awards and prize money of ₹ 10 lakh are given on April 24, the National Panchayati Raj Day.

4

Rajiv Gandhi Panchayat Sashaktikaran Abhiyan (RGPSA)

RGPSA has been launched during the Twelfth Five Year Plan (2012-17) period and subsumes the earlier smaller schemes of the Ministry of Panchayti Raj.

4.1 Objectives

RGPSA is envisaged to strengthen the panchayati raj system across the country and address critical gaps that constrain its success. RGPSA seeks to:

1. Enhance capacities and effectiveness of panchayats and the gram sabhas.
2. Enable democratic decision-making and accountability in panchayats and promote people's participation.
3. Strengthen the institutional structure for knowledge creation and capacity building of panchayats.
4. Promote devolution of powers and responsibilities to panchayats according to the spirit of the Constitution and PESA Act.
5. Strengthen gram sabhas to function effectively as the basic forum of people's participation, transparency and accountability within the panchayat system.
6. Create and strengthen democratic local self-government in areas where panchayats do not exist.
7. Strengthen the constitutionally mandated framework on which panchayats are founded.

The Centrally-sponsored Scheme of RGPSA has been launched taking into account the experiences learnt prior to its inception, lacunae felt in the effective implementation of the then existing schemes which aimed at strengthening the panchayati raj system in varying degrees. The emphasis previously was on strengthening the system by advocating greater devolution of 3Fs by States and in CSSs through systematic activity mapping and building the capacities of panchayat representatives and functionaries.

However, it was observed that there had been reluctance on the part of States as well as Central Ministries to devolve 3Fs usually citing the lack of capacity of panchayats as the reason. There was, also, grossly inadequate capacity building infrastructure and facilities. The involvement of gram sabhas as key units of governance, particularly in Schedule V Areas, also was at very low ebb. The panchayats lacked even most basic administrative and technical capacity to deal with the matters of revenue generation and maintenance of accounts in proper and required manner. Naturally owing to such factors, the quintessential element of functioning of panchayati raj system in desired manner, viz. the decentralised participatory grassroots level planning, suffered to a great extent.

The umbrella scheme of RGPSA provides for undertaking a lot of activities that can cope with many deficiencies including those referred to above. This scheme in fact has subsumed some of the erstwhile schemes of the Ministry of Panchayati Raj, namely Rasthriya Gram Swaraj Yojana (RGSY), Panchayat Mahila Evam Yuva Shakti Abhiyan (PMEYSA), Panchayat Empowerment Accountability Incentivisation Scheme (PEAIS), E-Panchayat and Resource Support to States (RSS). The other schemes in fact were being implemented up to the financial year 2012-13 also and had separate budgetary provision for the same. For 2012-13, the Plan provision under RGPSA was made only of a token nature i.e. ₹ 50 crore and out of this, financial assistance was provided to some States for certain identified activities only. The scheme of RGPSA, with absorption of the above mentioned schemes, came to be implemented in full swing w.e.f. the financial year 2013-14.

4.2 Modalities

Funds are accessed by States as per need-based and

context-specific plans selected from various activities permitted under RGPSA. RGPSA extends to all States and UTs of the country. The funding pattern in the scheme is 75:25 by Central and State Governments except for North-Eastern States, where it is 90:10.

States are required to fulfil some essential conditions for accessing any RGPSA funds which include the following:

1. Regular election to panchayats, or local bodies, in non-Part IX areas, under the superintendence and control of the SFC.
2. At least one-third reservation for women in panchayats or other local bodies.
3. Constitution of State Finance Commission (SFC) every five years, and placement of action taken report on the recommendations of the SFC in the State legislature.
4. Constitution of district planning committees (DPCs) in all districts, and issuing of guidelines/rules to make these functional.

States that do not fulfil the above essential conditions are not eligible for funds under RGPSA.

Strengthening the panchayati raj system involves not just provision of capital and human resource assets such as provision of expertise, buildings, training etc. but also adequate devolution, bottom-up planning, convergence, accountability and free and fair elections. Under RGPSA, States are expected to show appropriate progress on the above-mentioned aspects, as they access funding for various components under the scheme. These deliverables encompass the following:

1. Articulating an appropriate policy framework for providing administrative and technical support to panchayats, including recruitment and service rules as needed.
2. Strengthening the financial base of panchayats by assigning appropriate taxes, fees etc.
3. Timely release of Central Finance Commission (CFC)

grants, as untied grants and release of SFC grants.

4. Ensuring devolution of funds, functions and functionaries.
5. Preparing and operationalizing a framework for bottom-up grassroots planning and convergence through DPC.
6. Ensuring free and fair elections, and making the SEC autonomous.
7. Strengthening the institutional structure for capacity building of panchayats and selecting suitable partners for capacity building.
8. Strengthening gram sabhas, and creation of mahila sabhas and ward sabhas.
9. Institutionalizing accountability processes such as voluntary disclosure of information and social audit.
10. Strengthening the system of budgeting, accounts and audit, including use of e-enabled processes.
11. Ensuring compliance of State laws and rules with PESA.

4.3 Activities

Activities that can be undertaken by States in RGPSA for strengthening the panchayati raj institutions are as follows:

1. Provision of core staff at the gram panchayat (GP), keeping in mind the size of the panchayat and staff available.
2. New GP buildings, repairs of existing buildings, construction of toilets (including separate toilets for women), electricity and water supply for the GPs.
3. Capacity building and training for elected representatives and panchayat functionaries.
4. Strengthening of institutional structure for capacity building and training, including setting up of state panchayat resource centres (SPRCs), district panchayat resource centres and block resource centres.
5. Provision of computers to panchayats.
6. Resources to panchayats that lack resources for basic activities like gram sabha meetings, planning and social audit are supported under the scheme to carry out their

basic processes.

7. Special activities are supported in order to strengthen gram sabha in PESA areas and in North-Eastern areas where Part IX does not apply.
8. Innovative activities for strengthening panchayati raj may be included in State Plans for up to ₹ 2 crore per annum.
9. Information, education and communication (IEC) activities to raise the awareness level of panchayats are supported under the scheme.
10. Strengthening of State Election Commissions including purchase of electronic voting machines (EVMs), process development etc., in order to ensure free and fair elections to panchayats.
11. To support the panchayati raj departments of the States, programme management units (PMUs) at the State and district level are supported under the scheme. The PMUs help panchayati raj department in planning, implementation and monitoring of the scheme.

At the national level, the following activities are undertaken in RGPSA:

1. Performance assessment and incentivisation of panchayats through a rigorous process.
2. Support to resource agencies for innovative activities.
3. Technical support to States.

4.4 Integration with Swachh Bharat Mission

In view of the launching of Swachh Bharat Mission, an advisory on critical areas of convergence with RGPSA has been issued concretising the steps to be taken in this behalf under the scheme. Some of the points are as under:

1. Ensuring separate toilet each for male and female while constructing new GP bhawans.
2. Priority to provision of toilets (both for male and female) while taking up repair/upgradation of GPs.
3. Earmarking some funds for generating awareness on sanitation under IEC activity.

4. Adoption/preparation of module on sanitation by SIRDs for their annual training.

Though it is a new scheme, RGPSA has made an important intervention for strengthening the panchayati raj system in the country. To begin with, as States have prepared their plan proposals under the scheme, they have taken stock of the panchayati raj system, and set goals for strengthening it. Second, some key problems at the grassroots can now be addressed.

5

Economic, Social and Political Empowerment of Women

The extent of empowerment of women in the national hierarchy is determined largely by three factors: their economic, social and political identity. These factors are deeply intertwined and interlinked with many cross cutting linkages. However, if efforts in even one dimension remain absent or weak, outcomes generated by the other components are adversely affected. Women can be truly empowered only when all the three factors are simultaneously addressed and made compatible with each other. In other words, for holistic empowerment of women to happen, economic, social and political aspects impacting women's life must converge effectively.

It is a well-acknowledged fact that the thrust on social and human development is an important plank of next generation policy reforms. The efforts are being complemented by a steep jump in budgetary outlays for social sectors, along with dedicated initiatives for removing poverty and increasing employment. Participation of women in productive activities reduces poverty, enhances economic growth and hence benefits society at large.

5.1 Economic Empowerment

Women's lack of economic empowerment not only impedes growth and poverty reduction, but also has a host of other negative impacts including less favourable education and health outcomes for children. Thus, it is extremely important to ensure that women are economically empowered.

Women's contribution to the economy remains significantly invisible in national accounts. Although a certain degree of statistical invisibility of women in the economy is a global phenomenon, it is particularly predominant in India and other South Asian nations due to their orthodox socio-cultural milieu. The United Nations Statistical Division has been active in extending the production boundary of the Systems of National Accounts (SNA), 1993 and this has led to the inclusion of the unpaid work of women in the care economy in the national accounting system as satellite accounts. This extended production boundary of SNA, 1993 provides a better understanding of women's contribution to the economy.

5.1.1 Vicious Circle of Poverty and Gender Inequality: Poverty and gender inequality thrive on each other. In other words, there exists a two-way link between economic growth and poverty, and gender inequality. At one level, poverty and the lack of growth exacerbate gender disparities. Inequalities between girls and boys in access to schooling or adequate healthcare are more acute among poor people than among those with higher incomes. While poor people have less access to such productive resources as land and credit, poor women generally have the least access of all. Similarly, health and schooling of girls and women are more vulnerable to economic downturns than those of boys and men. At another level, gender inequalities undermine the prospects for poverty reduction in fundamental ways. While disparities in basic rights, access to schooling, credit and jobs, and the ability to participate in public life take their most direct toll on women and girls, the evidence shows that gender inequality ultimately hinders economic growth.

The rationale for economically empowering women is compelling both for its own sake and for other spillover benefits. Economic participation of women—their presence in the workforce in quantitative terms—is important not only for lowering the disproportionate levels of poverty among women, but also as an important step toward raising household income and encouraging economic development in a country. Education, employment and ownership rights of women have a powerful influence on their ability to control their environment and contribute to economic development.

However, participation alone is not enough because quality of women's work is also important. A key challenge is to overcome a situation where women may gain employment with relative ease, but where their employment is either concentrated in poorly paid or *unskilled job ghettos*, characterized by the absence of upward mobility and opportunity. For example, women are often concentrated in *feminized professions* such as nursing and teaching, office work, care of the elderly and disabled—termed *horizontal occupational segregation*—where they tend to remain in lower job categories than men. Since these activities are carried out by women, they are the lowest paid, in addition to offering limited or no opportunity for advancement. The term *feminization of poverty* is often used to illustrate the fact that a substantial percentage of poor are women and that the gap between women and men in poverty has not lessened, but may well have widened in recent years.

5.1.2 Gender Discrimination in Wages: Discriminatory practices in the labour market are reflected in the wages of women workers. They are not only concentrated in low-paid occupations in the unorganised sector but are subjected to discrimination in payment. In terms of wage-workers, for all categories of employment, considerable differentials prevail in both rural and urban areas. The increase in gender disparity in wages in the urban areas is quite marked and it usually results from employment of women in lower-paying activities in the aggregate. For the majority of women engaged in paid economic activity, the fact of being female means being paid less than men for their work. It is most evident in respect of agricultural labourers. Agricultural daily wages are in general low, though they vary by type of agricultural operation (ploughing, sowing, weeding, harvesting, etc.), by the prosperity of a state or region, and by gender. Some operations such as ploughing do not involve women at all, whereas others such as weeding are women-intensive.

From the various categories of industrial work, the manufacturing sector is the most discriminatory. Coupled with gender discrimination in wage differentials is inequality in access to superior positions and promotions. Men are seen confined to regular and more managerial or technically-oriented jobs while women are often given technically inferior positions where they are mostly hired as contract workers. Women get lower pay despite longer working hours and the conditions of work are sub-standard. Discrimination exists not only in terms of wages but also in terms of access to employment. Often, women are found concentrated in occupations where the wage rates, as well as working conditions, are poor and sub-standard.

The reasons for gender discrimination in wages may not be specific to India but the cultural context also is an important factor. The implicit assumptions that women should be paid less then men include the following: (a) low levels of skill on entry, (b) lack of access to on-the-job training, (c) employment histories punctuated by time spent bearing and raising children, (d) time off to care for family members and (e) the assumption that men are the primary earners.

5.1.3 Strategies for Economic Empowerment of Women: These are as under:

A. Sound Macroeconomic Policies: Gender inequalities are manifest as women and men have different access to resources, roles and responsibilities, both in the market and at the household. In the Indian context, fiscal policies are being increasingly examined through gender sensitive-budgeting exercises, although the focus still remains on expenditures in *soft sectors*, with several aspects like taxation, trade, capital flows etc. remaining largely an unstudied domain. Macroeconomic policies are formulated and implemented in areas such as trade, fiscal management, debt financing, social welfare and other sectors without a comprehensive assessment of their potential gender impacts. All these issues would be particularly important if the analysis of the sources of growth were to suggest that influencing the distribution of income and assets by gender might have a beneficial effect. Some policies—particularly those promoting health and education, or promoting greater women's property rights and control over assets or access to credit, technology, and transport—are likely to be win-win policies in terms of higher growth, greater gender equality, and reduced susceptibility of women to economic shock.

B. Improvement in Infrastructure: Development of infrastructure was previously assumed to be gender neutral, with both sexes benefiting equally from well-designed projects. The new thinking asserts that gender-responsive infrastructure interventions can free up women's time, thereby increasing girls' enrolment in schools and facilitating women's participation in income-generation and decision-making activities.

In the area of transport, men and women have varying transport needs and constraints and are affected differently by transport interventions. Rural transport projects that build roads for motorized transport often do not benefit rural women, who mainly work in and around the village and travel on foot. Urban transport systems that transport people to and from employment centres are sometimes inadequate for women, who must combine income-generating activities with household and familial activities, such as taking children to school and health centres and visiting the market. Poor women, who balance productive, social, and reproductive roles in societies, often have higher demands on their time than poor men.

There are women-specific transport needs like transportation of primary products; inter- and intra-village roads/paths; non-motorised transport; dedicated bicycle lanes, pedestrian sidewalk use, passenger safety, and so on which should be included in any transport policy or plan. Every major transport project should undertake a pre-project gender assessment survey to ensure that women's needs are addressed right at the design and planning level. Project planning and implementation need to be participatory, including community infrastructure management and maintenance.

Design improvements are necessary to meet the specific needs of women, especially lower height of entry steps, length of straps, and so on in buses and trains, installation of handrails, ramps, and so on. Dedicated exclusive services such as ladies special buses and trains are also necessary. Women's needs require better route planning. The provision of special buses, increased services for women travelling during off-peak hours or services on less-travelled routes all need more attention due to personal security risks at parking lots, buses, bus stops, airports, highways etc. A gender audit of transport terminals must be undertaken and safety measures for women introduced.

C. Gender-sensitive Agricultural Policies: Rural women form the most important productive workforce in the Indian economy. Beyond the conventional market-oriented narrower definition of *productive workers*, almost all women in rural India can be considered as *farmers* in some sense, working as agricultural labourers, unpaid workers in the family farm enterprise, or combination of the two. Moreover, several farm activities traditionally carried out by men are also being undertaken by women as men are pulled away into higher paying employment. Thus, rural India is witnessing a process which could be described as feminization of agriculture.

Despite significant contribution of women in the production process, an all pervasive bias of development planners in treating them primarily as consumers of social services rather than producers, kept them away from the development programmes in agriculture and allied sectors. As men and women have different roles and needs and face gender-specific constraints, women may not automatically benefit from development activities, but may remain excluded.

In spite of the key role of women in crop husbandry,

animal husbandry, fisheries, forestry and post-harvest technology, those incharge of formulating packages of technologies, services and public policies for rural areas have often tended to neglect the productive role of women. Consequently, the developments in technologies, specifically tailored to women-specific occupations and the involvement of women in technology development and transfer have received inadequate attention from both scientific and administrative departments of the Government.

Women have traditionally been discriminated in their access to productive resources and have been denied ownership of land, cattle, trees, harvest and shelter. They have even been discriminated in access to credit and marketing facilities for their economic activities. It is, thus, essential to develop strategies and mechanism to improve women's access to agricultural support services.

It has been recognized that for an accelerated socio-economic development of any community, the active participation of women in the entire process is very essential. In a social set up like ours, the participation of women in the development process has to be ensured through tangible measures, taken at various levels, which result in empowerment of women in the real sense. In view of the above, government has taken a conscious view to make adequate provisions in its policies and programmes through which it is to be ensured that the women of the country are empowered and they become the active participants in the development process.

The absence of faster diversification is partly due to the lack of new economic opportunities for women. While men migrate as well as take up new employment opportunities in rural areas, women find themselves at a disadvantage.

There appears to be a faster rate of occupational mobility out of agriculture among men than among women. The latter remain more bound to rural areas and to agriculture due to socio-cultural and structural causes.

D. Self-help Groups (SHGs) and Empowerment of Women: The emergence and rapid multiplication of self-help groups (SHGs) based on micro credit is a phenomenon that is gaining increasing importance in the development scenario. SHGs are being viewed by governments and NGOs as a strategy for both women's empowerment as well as poverty reduction. SHGs are a conduit for routing a wide range of government-sponsored development messages and schemes. NGOs have increasingly been adopting SHGs as a strategy to bring women together, at a faster pace and larger scale than the collective building processes adopted by them earlier. A number of powerful players like MFIs, NGOs, corporations and donors—all of whom have a significant and growing interest in the SHG phenomenon which centres on poor women—have entered the arena. Credit is a right that poor women must have access to.

The experience of SHGs has shown that they have provided improved access to credit. Poor women are now perceived by the mainstream financial sector as creditworthy. Women have used savings and credit for needs such as those related to education and health, and in particular for crisis related needs. Participation in SHGs has meant opportunities related to mobility and a legitimate space in the public realm for leaders of SHGs. Notwithstanding all the positive achievements, the overall picture is uneven and raises following concerns related to gender justice and livelihoods:

1. Despite the increased access to credit, there continue to be several hurdles faced by women when they want to access credit from banks. These include huge amounts of paperwork and the fact that women are often pressurized by banks to recover loans made earlier to men in the village as an unwritten conditionality before loans are released to them.
2. It is increasingly being reported that SHG members have limited control over financial resources that they borrow despite being the conduit for access to such credit through

their groups. The burden of repayment of such loans falls almost exclusively on the women. As SHGs are almost exclusively women-only, often women become proxy to husband's demands without the men taking up the responsibility for repayment or proper utilization of these loans.

3. Many of the micro enterprise activities undertaken have tended to be unviable. Low levels of credit absorption capacity, low skill base and low asset base have been challenges to the SHG movement, which are yet to be addressed. Moreover, lack of skills, experience and technical support services to promote livelihoods and build sustainable interventions among the intermediary organizations especially NGOs etc. does not enable sustainable livelihood options to be developed.
4. Access to credit as the focus of the micro credit programmes looses sight of the fundamental issues of access and control over common resources such as water, forests etc. which are the mainstay of occupations of a large number of the rural poor. The fundamental livelihood concerns related to the existing economic realities of poor women's lives remain largely unaddressed in the process.

E. Skill Development: With the advent of globalisation and liberalization, new technologies and fast changing markets tend to make existing skills obsolete, requiring upgradation of existing skills and adoption of new skills and multi-skilling. Globalisation often puts a premium on skills, requiring high levels of education, often out of the reach of the unorganised sector workers. On the other hand, it opens up new markets which workers can reach by adopting existing or traditional skills.

Women workers are usually at the lowest-paid end of any sector. They are usually termed as unskilled, even though very often their work, though low-paid, requires a certain level of technique. Furthermore, many of the skills that women learn are those that are in some way connected to care and reproduction, which are often not regarded as skills at all. For example, women in forest areas have a skill of recognizing and using herbal plants. However, this skill is not regarded as skill at all, either by the person who is documenting the skills, or even by the women themselves.

Similarly, the potential marketability of a particular skill is never recognized. This refers to a woman's skills which currently are not being marketed but which have a good market potential like embroidery or knowledge of herbs. The *care skills* of the women can no longer be sidelined. These would include knowledge of child-care, care of the sick and particular skills such as mid-wifery. One unfortunate tendency that has been noticed in the desperate search for employment that goes on in the unorganised sector is the tendency towards deskilling. Workers lose their traditional or acquired skills when they cannot find employment with these skills.

5.2 Social Empowerment

5.2.1 Women and Health: Discrimination against women and girls impinges upon their right to health and manifests itself in the form of worsening health and nutrition indices. Thus, India continues to grapple with unacceptably high maternal mortality rate (MMR), infant mortality rate (IMR) and increasing rates of anaemia, malnutrition, HIV/AIDS among women.

Women also disproportionately lack access to health services. Inaccessibility of health centres and poverty prevent them from getting timely medical aid. Absence of toilets and drinking water adversely impacts their health.

Inadequacies of clean cooking fuels adversely impacts women and children's work burden, health and nutrition.

Women and girls spend a great deal of time gathering fuel, adversely affecting their productivity and education. Use of firewood and inferior fuels such as weeds or crop wastes leads to smoke-related ailments including respiratory diseases, cancer and cataracts resulting in blindness.

Women and girls in India face a crisis of growing health needs. From the moment of conception to the end of life, the challenges to the female sex are enormous, especially those who are poor; suffer from multiple exclusions, including caste, class, geographic isolation and tribal status. Health policies have few specific strategies for improving access to marginalized groups.

Malnutrition begins during infancy and sets in motion a life long cycle of poor health. Over half of all Indian women suffer from anaemia, which acerbates maternal morbidity. More women die of maternal death related causes in India than in any other country in the world. Women as a whole are especially susceptible to many diseases because of their poor nutritional standards and discriminatory practices in health inputs right from their birth.

Furthermore, every form of violence against women has steadily increased including rapes, dowry murder and domestic violence. Despite the alarming health crisis of women and girls, the national policy focus prioritizes family planning and reproductive health without addressing underlying issues such as women's low participation in decision-making, which adversely affects their health status. It is noteworthy that the leading killer of women in India is tuberculosis. Yet due to the focus on maternal and reproductive health this fact is little known and there are no gender-specific policies or programmes in place with regard to this disease.

5.2.2 Women and Education: There is an increased awareness that education is one of the most valuable means of achieving gender equality and the empowerment of women. Education is seen as a critical factor in breaking the inter-generational cycle of transmission of poverty. The power of education lies not just in imparting formal literacy, but rather in the acquisition of skills that enable access to multiple literacy—economic, legal, health, political and media etc.

Education is a key intervention in initiating and sustaining processes of empowerment. Good quality education can help women and marginalized communities to: (a) improve their status, (b) enable them to have greater access to information and resources and (c) challenge various forms of discrimination. Education helps strengthen democratic processes as it allows for greater and more equitable participation. Being educated leads to greater self-confidence and self-esteem. It enables engagement with development processes and institutions of governance from a position of strength. Poor women from socially disadvantaged communities are invariably not literate and therefore find themselves at a disadvantage when participating in development processes.

It is, however, important to recognise that while being literate or educated is necessary for empowerment, it does not automatically ensure it. For that, a society needs an education system which is of good quality and promotes critical thinking. From the perspective of gender, this means that education and literacy should enable women and girls to critically analyse their situations, raise questions about their subordination and help them make informed choices. It is well-known that the institution of schooling is an important site for socialisation that actually reinforces rather than challenges patriarchy and gender discrimination. It is in this context that the content and pedagogy of education become critical considerations.

The focus of educational planning is generally on formal education but this is only one dimension of the educational provisioning, especially when needs of deprived women are under consideration and empowerment of women is the main objective.

5.2.3 Women and Media: Media plays a critical role in changing gender stereotypes. The approach to media strategy in India has been to use it as an instrument of change and to control its possible misuse. Media is encouraged to develop a code of conduct, professional guidelines, other self-regulatory mechanisms to remove gender stereotypes and promote a balanced portrayal of women and men.

The existing law on regulating content in the media is

contained in different sources. Thus, Article 51A of the Constitution states that it shall be the duty of every citizen of India to renounce practices derogatory to the dignity of women. Similarly, Section 294 of the IPC provides for penalties for obscene acts or conduct. The Indecent Representation of Women (Prohibition) Act, 1986 prohibits indecent representation of women through advertisement or in publications, writings, paintings, figures or in any other manner. The Act was enacted in the year 1986 and since then the issue of what is *obscene* has been a subject of great debate. The Act itself mostly revolves around how the object will affect society and the public morality rather than how it offends women.

The Indian Information Technology Act, 2000 has declared online pornography a punishable offence.

The role of the media in portraying women and the female gender as a whole leaves much to be desired. Press and the print media are generally found to unduly sensationalize traumatic events such as rape etc. thereby invading the privacy of the victim. Very few positive stories of girls/women are published who have stood up for their rights or are achievers. Similarly, the electronic media and films portray serial/films highly derogatory to women, glorifying subservience of the woman to her husband/in-laws, celebrating the birth of the boy child and portraying the disappointments of the family at the birth of the girl child. Eve teasing/sexual harassment is often a *fun* item in Indian films. As a result the general populace is fed on a regular diet of stories/news that are highly gender abusive, thus reinforcing traditional views that the women are an inferior race and can be freely exploited.

The media has perforce to become gender sensitive and more responsible when portraying women and thus play a significant role in bringing about attitudinal changes in the society. A gender-friendly media policy needs to be formulated for this purpose.

Negative, violent and/or degrading images of women

including pornography, stereotyped portrayals, have increased in different forms using new communication technologies in some instances, and bias against women remains in the media. Poverty, the lack of access and opportunities, illiteracy, lack of computer literacy and language barriers, prevent women from using the information and communication technologies, including the internet. Development of and access to internet infrastructure is limited especially in developing countries and particularly for women.

The lack of gender sensitivity in the media is evidenced by the failure to eliminate the gender-based stereotyping and the reinforcement of women's traditional role that can be found in public and private media. The continued projection of negative and degrading images of women in media communications is evident. The worldwide trend towards consumerism has created a climate in which advertisements and commercial messages often portray women primarily as consumers and target girls and women of all ages inappropriately. Advertisements of beauty products, magazines and beauty pageants mushrooming all over have led to the creation of an image of an *ideal woman.*

Media policy needs to be gender proactive. There is a need to encourage media to project positive images and balanced portrayal of women and girls to enable attitudinal changes. The media policy should also help in generating awareness on gender issues and concerns so that the process of societal reorientation towards creating a gender just society gets widely disseminated.

5.3 Political Empowerment

In the early years of the Independence of India in 1947, much of the country's governance was in the hands of elected representatives and the official machinery. Such a centralized approach did not produce desired results, especially in terms of the inclusion of marginalized groups within the governance processes. Constitutional, legislative and policy reforms since then and the continued administrative decentralization have increased the political participation of marginalized groups, especially poor women. Women's increased political participation has yielded positive results. Issues central to development—including health, nutrition, family income and education—have taken centre stage as women participate in panchayati raj institutions (PRI), village development boards and other governance structures.

There has been growing acceptance of the importance to society of the full participation of women in decision-making and power at all levels and in all fora, including inter-governmental, governmental, and non-governmental sectors. In some countries, women have also attained higher positions in these spheres. An increasing number of countries applied affirmative and positive action policies, including quota systems or voluntary agreements in some countries, measurable goals and targets, developed training programmes for women's leadership and introduced measures to reconcile family and work responsibilities of both women and men. National mechanisms and machineries for the advancement of women as well as national and international networks of women politicians, parliamentarians, activists and professionals in various fields have been established or upgraded and strengthened.

Despite general acceptance of the need for a gender balance in decision-making bodies at all levels, a gap between *de jure* and *de facto* equality has persisted. Notwithstanding substantial improvements of *de jure* equality between women and men, the actual participation of women at the highest levels of national and international decision-making has not significantly changed and gross under-representation of women in decision-making bodies in all areas, including *inter alia* politics, conflict prevention and resolution mechanisms, the economy, the environment and the media hinders the inclusion of a gender perspective in these critical spheres of influence. Women continue to be underrepresented at the legislative, ministerial and sub-ministerial levels, as well as at the highest levels of the corporate sector and other social and economic institutions. Traditionally assigned gender roles limit women's choices in education and careers and compel women to assume the burden for household responsibilities.

Initiatives and programmes aimed at women's increased participation in decision-making are hindered by a host of factors, among which the following are prominent:

1. Lack of human and financial resources for training and advocacy for political careers.
2. Gender-sensitive attitudes towards women in the society.
3. Lack of accountability of elected officials and political parties for promoting gender equality and women's participation in public life.
4. Lack of social awareness of the importance of balanced participation of women and men in decision-making.
5. Lack of willingness on the part of men to share power; sufficient dialogue and co-operation with women's non-governmental organizations, along with organizational and political structures, which enable all women to participate in all spheres of political decision-making.

While the planning process and public expenditure in terms of programmes and schemes are sought to be included in gender budgeting, yet without gender sensitivity of important organs such as police and judiciary, the implementation will not be successful. This is especially true of schemes which have a strong element of protection or are rights based. For example, if a woman is not given her due share of property or other assets as per law, it is essential that these agencies help and support her in getting her share without much delay or harassment. This can happen only if gender sensitivity is inculcated in such bodies and they are made aware of the laws, policies, programmes and other initiatives for women. It is also important that justice delivery is quick with the enforcement machinery being responsive and gender sensitive to women's needs especially in cases of domestic violence and personal assault.

It is, therefore, necessary to induct a larger number of women in these bodies at different levels. This will encourage women to actively participate in power sharing and active participation in decision-making. Efforts should be made to provide coaching facilities and support services so that women can compete along with men both at entry level and to facilitate upward mobility of women in these institutions.

The setting up of women police stations, women's help desk in every police station, and increasing the strength of women police to 30 percent of the total force has been reiterated a number of times by the Ministry of Women and Child Development in a number of forums. The Ministry of Home Affairs should take requisite steps to fulfil their obligations towards gender budgeting by engendering the police force.

True, efforts have been made to empower women economically, socially, and politically, but as a result of the lack of synergy or coordination between these activities, the outcomes are not satisfactory. For example the increasing induction of women representatives into the PRIs should have meant automatic improvement in the lives of rural women, but if it has not happened, it is because the elected women were not educated or literate or even made aware of their rights. Also there are many groups of women who on account of tradition, culture, ethnic, social or religious background are more vulnerable compared to the women in the mainstream sector.

It is imperative that an integrated policy and strategy be formulated that addresses economic, social, and political empowerment simultaneously and holistically along with the requisite programmes and schemes. Once such a comprehensive policy and programs flowing from it are put in place, it will be possible to enable an all round development of women, which will usher in true empowerment.

To sum up, notable constitutional, legislative and policy reforms, and continued administrative decentralization have demonstrated the commitment of Governments (Centre and States) to increase political participation of women at grassroots level. Although only one-third of seats were reserved for women by the Seventy-third and Seventy-fourth constitutional amendments, the actual representation is higher at all levels. Increased political participation of women has yielded a range of positive results, not only for women but also for their families and communities. Central issues in development such as health, nutrition, family income and education are finding their way to the top of the agenda for action. Women's participation brings about more inclusive governance and effective community-cantered development.

6

Women Representation in PRIs

The Constitution prescribes only a minimum level of reservation of one-third for women in panchayats but the States have the leeway to mandate more than that level. Bihar took the bold step of reserving 50 percent of the panchayat seats for women. Currently, elected women representatives are in place in 54 percent of seats in Bihar's panchayats. Bihar's example was followed by Sikkim, which increased the reservations for women to 40 percent and held the elections under the new arrangement in January 2008. Chhattisgarh, Madhya Pradesh, Rajasthan and Uttarakhand have passed laws increasing the reservations for women in panchayats to 50 percent. About 1 million women have come out of their homes for the first time in centuries to hold public offices and to participate in public activities after Seventy-third Constitutional Amendment Act. This has been the most effective formal step towards political empowerment of women.

6.1 Representation of Marginalized Sections

It is a known fact that 40 percent of the elected women represent the marginalized sections and about 70 percent women representatives are illiterate and most of them have no previous political experience. Therefore, it is but natural that there is a widespread apprehension that women will be manipulated by men. However, in spite of several instances of such manipulation and capitulation by women, the presence of such a large number of women in panchayats has indeed had a deep impact on gender equity. The occupation of the marginalized women of elected seats and chairperson's posts in grassroots democracy is a huge social and political revolution, the significance of which would take at least a generation to fully unfold.

There can be no greater evidence for the fact that not only has panchayati raj attracted women to politics in large numbers, but also that the wish to contest for elections seems to be most keenly felt among the women belonging to the SCs and STs. Approximately 85.8 percent of all representatives surveyed were first-timers in panchayats, while 14.3 percent had been elected for a second or third term. That reservation has been critical to the representation of disadvantaged groups is confirmed by the fact that 88 percent of them were elected on reserved seats. By contesting and getting elected to PRIs, women have shattered the saga of their own submissiveness—that women are not willing to enter politics. For women, successful grassroots experience has meant a chance to form eloquent voice, to be heard and to make a difference in their communities.

Added to this is the fact that the women who have come under reservation have come in with their social and economic disadvantages, mostly non-literate, with little productive assets, largely dependent on wage labour and into a rural society that has fixed places for various castes and gender. These cannot be changed by a wave of the constitutional amendment wand.

In fact, gender as a phenomenon hardly ever appears in a pure form. It is almost always alloyed with caste, class and religious factors. In matters where there are clashes between gender and caste or class, it is impossible to expect women to align themselves with other women, going against their caste or class loyalties.

6.2 Image Building by Women

Some women have developed political ambitions too, especially when it is seen as a quick means for upward mobility. And political survival will be difficult if they betray class and caste interests. This is why the reservation of the post of president to the SC/ST category is so resented. The problem is in society, not in the panchayat that only reflects social reality.

Results from a nationwide survey of women's participation in panchayats suggest that a majority of the elected women representatives (EWRs) report an enhancement in their personal effectiveness and image after being elected. They also report a reduction in household responsibilities. There are many instances of EWR of the panchayat taking a keen interest and playing a significant role in the workings of grassroots politics. It has often been observed that women prioritize those developmental needs that seem to be more pressing from their perspective. EWRs have initiated work on plans of bringing in piped water in the village and also to build schools as against infrastructural development favoured by men.

There are number of success stories where EWRs of the panchayats have taken the lead in making efforts for smokeless stoves, crèches, community halls, and have taken the initiative in family and matrimonial matters, counselling of abusive and/or alcoholic husbands. Women are also seen to be more involved in monitoring the presence of teachers and medical staff in the school or health centre, and inspecting nutrition centres under the Integrated Child Development Scheme. Sometimes, women-headed panchayats have even experienced a dramatic increase in their revenues, sponsoring the auction of village ponds, community forests and village markets for the larger welfare of the community.

6.3 Role of Reservation for Women

It is for sure that without the system of reservation, women would have had no role to play in grassroots politics in India. As statistics show, 95 percent of women claimed they would never come to acquire positions in panchayats, if there were no provision of reserving seats for them. Reservation has at least succeeded in bringing the womenfolk in rural India into the political forum and elected women could now imagine standing against men in future. The successful EWR, now act as a kind of role models for the others. The increased proportion of the EWR has ensured the principles of justice between the sexes and this has certainly led to the fulfilment of certain interests of women, which may otherwise be neglected.

However, women's representation and presence in panchayats has continued to be influenced by the same ideology and tokenism as has continued at other political levels despite the political equality guaranteed by the Constitution. Women's representation in the decision-making positions with monitoring power is still negligible. The present rules of the game and decision-making procedure do not allow a greater participation of women and in the absence of women, there is no effort to recognize or change the game. The very absence of women at these levels thus leads to preservation and reinforcement of male-oriented and male benefiting types of decisions. Women's low self-esteem at the household level and their new role in local politics where they are now expected to function as leader creates a contradiction between women's role at home and in local government.

If reservations for women in PRIs are to lead to their empowerment in real terms, social, economic and political conditions which facilitate and encourage their participation, need to be created. As with most matters of empowerment, mere political will and articulation of policies alone will not translate into benefits for women. The translation into sensitive implementation would require changes in administrative and social structures. Moreover, a collaborative approach between the household, the community, the state, voluntary organizations and the media needs to be developed. The approach must also be multi-pronged, taking into account policies, laws, judicial processes, attitudes and social imaging of women.

Reservation has emerged as an important motivator (43 percent) for contesting the first election as much as its withdrawal was an important reason for not contesting the election among former women representatives (39 percent). By all accounts, particularly with each election round, it is clear that women have certainly made their presence in the power struggles once dominated by men. The increased proportion of the EWR has ensured the principles of justice between the sexes and this has certainly led to the fulfilment of certain interests of women, which may otherwise be neglected

Seventy-third Constitutional Amendment has opened up vistas of opportunities for women to prove their significant role in the development process. The entry of women has deep impact on gender equity. They have certainly made their presence in the power struggles once dominated by men. The amendment has made the *space* for these groups to enter the PRIs, the alacrity with which they take to the new role will vary. Women and challenges are almost synonymous terms. As the Indian society is not very open for women, they face challenges both at the political and social levels. There is a need for free flow of information to the women members of the panchayats, building a system by which the members of PRIs can exchange data and information, building the capability of the members/functionaries of PRIs to build and sustain alliances to take forward issues of governance at local level. The opportunities predominantly relate to raising issues and participating in decision-making process.

7

Illusion of Inclusion

7.1 Surrogate Participation

The issue of surrogate participation of women is one of those popular notions that just refuse to fade away. Yes, in some circumstances, where cultural and the social system is highly patriarchal, proxy participation continues. However, in circumstances where surrogate participation is seen, the actual situation might be that a man might be playing a nurturing and consulting role, assisting the new woman entrant into the panchayats. Further, while surrogate participation might exist for the first elected term of the women, quite often we come across situations where women have increasingly asserted themselves, once they have gained confidence—even winning the next election on their own worth, rather than as symbols of their male backers.

Heroic tales of women battling the odds abound in media reports and research studies. It is no accident that many of these accounts are from those States where the panchayat system is weak and neglected. Very often these individuals are heroes because of defective panchayati raj. On the other hand, in States where the framework of panchayati raj provides a nurturing environment for grassroots empowerment and does not inhibit it, one finds a larger scope for people to function effectively, without having to resort to heroism.

In fact, there are fewer odds to battle, in these States. In such States, since panchayati raj itself is a winner, those within it are all winners, in some measure or the other. Unfortunately, research in the functioning of panchayati raj often falls prey to anecdotes. Most studies have very low value as they often have poor sample sizes and biases of researchers, both positive and negative, creeping into the conclusions. Finally, constitutionally mandated panchayati raj is too young to throw up time series analysis of any great value.

Women's effective participation in the panchayati raj or the latter's usefulness for women's rights and development will become a reality only if panchayat system itself operates in a principled, self-governing, and significant way. It is important to strengthen the system and involve greater people's participation. Panchayati raj is often a charade in several States and political rhetoric hides their marginalization. One needs to analyse why such a widespread negative impression about PRIs has taken roots. Much of it is a matter of selective memory and autosuggestion—ignore the good stories and highlight the bad.

7.2 Panchayats versus Higher Level Governments

The functioning of panchayats is quite distinct from that of higher level governments. First, being closer to the people, a lot more corruption gets exposed to public view and compared to corruption at higher levels. Second, while grassroots level institutions have distinct advantages in localizing government, they also face proximate political and social pressures that make traditional virtues of public administration such as impartiality, neutrality and anonymity, difficult to realize locally. Third, regardless of whether PRIs are elected on a party basis or otherwise, they are political institutions. Elected members have constituencies both in the geographical and socio-political sense. One cannot avoid legitimate aspirations to nurse constituencies in today's context of highly competitive electoral politics and one must accept that there is bound to be a tendency to favour a region, a group of people or even individuals in developmental decision-making. Fourth, unlike legislators, PRI elected representatives are vested with executive authority and are empowered to take decisions having financial implications and authorize expenditure from public funds, decide levels of taxation, exercise power of collecting taxes and regulatory powers which are of a quasi-judicial character.

Two things need to be done to make panchayats more inclusive and effective as local governments. First, inclusiveness has meaning only if panchayats are given responsibilities in the letter and spirit of the Constitution. Unfortunately, panchayati raj is often a charade in several States and political rhetoric hides their marginalization. Both the Centre and the States need to bring in real devolution, which can be differentiated from the charade that panchayati raj has often become (Table 7.1).

Table 7.1: Real versus Not-so-real Devolution

Real Devolution	Not-so-real Devolution
Clear role assignment.	Somebody else (above or below) responsible for panchayat performance.
Power to spend money; power to tax	Limited power to collect resources.
Discretion in spending money.	Scheme bound expenditure.
Power to hire-fire and control staff.	Staff owned and assigned by higher level governments.
Direct accountability.	Somebody else (above or below) acting for the panchayats.

Second, decision-making processes in panchayats need to be better defined, to diminish the possibility of elite capture, proxy participation, single point decision-making and corruption. The formula for improving PRI functioning would follow a four-fold path; simplify, inform, review and hold accountable for non-performance or mal-administration. Some key steps in this regard are as follows.

7.3 Essentials for Democratic Functioning of PRIs

There are 8 inter-linked aspects of ensuring that PRIs work more democratically:

1. The emphasis on consensus in decision-making should be

approached with caution. While true consensus is appreciable, an unnecessary emphasis on consensus could stunt the growth of democracy. Consensus undermines democracy in two ways: first, in a consensus, the strongest voices prevail automatically. Thus, it is easier for a situation of elite capture to prevail if business rules of representative bodies expressly prefer consensus in decision-making. Reservations in favour of women and the socially disadvantaged do not make much sense in a consensus situation because one can just as easily silence the poor. The second disadvantage of a consensus situation is that elected representatives can hide behind a consensus decision to avoid responsibility and accountability towards their voters. Therefore, votes have always to be recorded. This is an important aspect of democratic PRI functioning. If there is a consensus or unanimity, even this should be recorded. The record of voting by individual members in PRI meetings could become the most important mechanism of opening up the proceedings to the public, particularly if there is express provision in the law for disclosing the voting pattern to the public. Mandatory public display of resolutions of the PRIs along with the record of members voting for or against them will enable the public to know what their members are doing for them. They will know how their members have articulated their concerns in meetings. More than anything else, this alone will be an effective mechanism of downward accountability.

2. Procedures for conduct of meetings will have to be laid may be necessary, in order to ensure that those who do not feel up to articulating their concerns in an open meeting can still make their presence felt in decision-making.
3. A strict quorum requirement will diminish the scope of marginalization in decision-making.
4. Ensure that the body is collectively responsible for its actions. The requirement of collective responsibility is

another method of increasing accountability of the body to the people. Once a member knows that his position is also in jeopardy as he is also vicariously responsible for wrong acts of his colleague-members in the body, there is a greater price to be paid for being a passive spectator to the proceedings. Members will be induced to participate meaningfully and there will be peer pressure on each other not to take wrong decisions.

5. Make decision-making committee-based. Most panchayat legislations provide for standing committees in panchayats, but these provisions are neglected and hardly operatonalised. Committee-based decision-making diminishes the scope for elite capture and allows for the articulation of all voices.
6. Put in place mechanisms to open up the process of decision-making for public gaze. Ordinarily, meetings shall be open to the public. There must be full disclosure of facts in meetings, so that reasoned decisions can be taken. One method of doing this is to ensure a prior circulation of the agenda for a meeting and if necessary, allow one meeting to intervene before a decision is made. Thus, a resolution can be introduced in a particular meeting and discussed, but voting could be held in the next meeting of the body.
7. Intervals between the rotation of reservations for women and SC and ST representatives need to be extended. If reservations are rotated after every 5 year term, it leaves very little incentive for the members elected on a reserved seat to perform, because he or she knows that next time around, there will only be a remote chance of being elected as she will not have the benefit of reservation in the same seat.
8. Provide a right to recourse to an independent institutional mechanism that gives speedy relief to the aggrieved—effectively bolstering empowerment through panchayats. With greater devolution and decentralization, there will be

a need to investigate independently complaints made by individuals, groups and even the Government relating to defective administration by local bodies. An ombudsman system could provide a convenient and relatively low-cost mechanism to deal with complaints of mal-administration.

7.4 Gram Sabha Meetings

The women participation may not be greatly enthusiastic right now but it will definitely be watched in future. The difficulty of many elected women representatives (EWRs) to change their age-old customs and practices is an important reason for their being not effective in delivering development. As women are still considered one of the neglected categories in some of the regions of India, there should be a separate quorum for attendance of women and for attendance at gram sabha meetings. In view of the crucial importance of adequate women's participation in meetings of the gram sabha, a sub-quorum of female attendance should be built into the required quorum.

Moreover, provision may be made that meetings of the gram sabha be preceded by meetings of the mahila sabha, comprising all adult women voters of the village panchayat to ensure that gender concerns and preferences get fully reflected in the proceedings of the gram sabha. In addition to that, each village should have a mahila mandal and a mahila sabha and efforts should be made to facilitate raising of women's concerns in meetings of gram sabhas and ward sabhas. Political parties and social activists should be encouraged to create greater awareness among the women about the importance of PRIs and the need for active participation in gram sabha meetings. There should be a provision of women component plans in PRI budgets. There should be a linkgage between self-help groups and PRIs at all levels. Women candidates should be given an opportunity to serve full term. Even education cannot make much difference unless training regarding the rules of panchayati raj is imparted.

7.5 Training for Women

There must be special training for women at the gram sabha level as women hardly get any training for capacity building. Most of them are ignorant about their rights and responsibilities to function as people's representatives in a democratic system. We have training facilities and several training institutions. A lot more thinking has to be put in the content and methodology of training.

Women in the villages suffer from lack of mobility and interaction. At initial stages, the first comers need family support and help from friends and community. But eventually, they can be on their own. Panchayats must be seen as a nursery of leadership for women. The women from the tribal and dalit communities need very special training for empowerment. They need special institutions for the same. But till today, there are no institutions for this. To change the patriarchal mindset of our communities, we have to create special awareness programmes for the society as a whole.

If reservations for women in panchayati raj institutions are to lead to their empowerment in real terms, social, economic and political conditions which facilitate and encourage their participation needs to be created. As with most matters of empowerment, mere political will and articulation of policies will not alone translate into benefits for women. The translation into sensitive implementation would require changes in administrative and social structures. Moreover, a collaborative approach between the household, the community, the State, voluntary organizations and the media needs to be developed. The approach must also be multi-pronged, taking into account policies, laws, judicial processes, attitudes and social imaging of women.

Just as in the case of most government offices, a thick veil of secrecy hides inefficiencies, arbitrariness, corruption and nepotism from public gaze in PRIs too. An example of the secrecy that surrounds executive action in PRIs is seen in the selection of beneficiaries for various schemes. The logical transparent sequence ought to be the laying down of the selection criteria, publicising them, calling for applications through the gram sabha, processing them with reference to the criteria, making selections and ending with publicly explaining the rationale of the selection made. When there is a great deal of arbitrariness in decision-making at the local level, records will not show how the choice was arrived at or whether various options and possibilities were analysed and on which criteria the final decision was made. Fairness at the cutting edge will need to be seen and corroborated by full disclosure, whatever may be the inconvenience and cost involved for the administration.

Therefore, systems that ensure easy access for the citizen to information must be put in place. If the right to information is to have any meaning, information will have to be systematised and packaged in a manner that makes sense to those who seek it.

8

Opportunities and Challenges for Women in PRIs

The experiences of women in the PRIs have been so varied, across the three levels of the PRIs and the different states that except for some "tautological" statements little can be said. We need to differentiate the women who hail from families with political background and those who can be termed *first generation political aspirants*—women who drifted into PRIs due to the Seventy-third amendment. Even though the amendment made the "space" for both these groups to enter the PRIs, the alacrity with which they take to the new role will vary. This is to be noted that hitherto, space for women to participate in institutions like the PRI, which are in the "public sphere", were negligible. Consequently, the early entrants have had only "male role models" of political leadership. Thus, we have had women in a double blind—to be seen as effective, they have to take to masculine ways and when they do that they cease representing women's interests.

From everywhere, an often-heard comment is that many of these women would not like to contest in the next round of elections. Why is that so? Is it a pointer to their "unsuitability" to assume leadership? Or an inability to cope with multiple and conflicting role demands? Or is it time to ask ourselves what is it about PRIs (and politics) that makes it unpalatable to half of humanity, even when it can determine the quality of life. Added to this is the fact that the women who have come under reservation have come in with their social and economic disadvantages—mostly non-literate, with little productive assets, largely dependent on wage labour and in rural society that has fixed places for various castes and gender. These cannot be changed by a wave of the constitutional amendment wand.

8.1 Opportunities for Women

It is recognised that the Seventy-third Constitutional Amendment has opened up vistas of opportunities for women to prove their significant role in the development process. The fact that women are in PRIs itself is an enabling factor for women. And that women are in PRIs in a particular percentage is even more enabling. However, the scope for opportunities does not limit itself to reservations alone. Against this backdrop, some of the opportunities have been identified below.

1. 33 percent reservation in panchayats.
2. Participation in national level discussions/events.
3. Raising women's issues in panchayat (like lack of access to water, health, electricity etc.).
4. Opportunities to take up issues specific to women and children.
5. Taking decisions in development of panchayats.
6. Opportunities provided by gram sabhas—an occasion for large number of women to participate and raise their concerns.
7. Establishing relationship between public and women representatives.
8. Opportunity in proper identification of BPL families.
9. Creating women SHGs through women panchayat members.
10. Opportunity for women presidents to express their views and ideas.

Through the implementation of 33 percent reservation in panchayats, women have got an opportunity to raise their concerns and opinion in gram sabha. The opportunity of establishing a relationship with the public (ranked as second) is also considered a big boon to the participants. Thus, the opportunities predominantly relate to raising issues and participating in decision-making process. The women can participate in decision-making process for providing basic services to the masses. Nevertheless, women in PRIs still lack the capacity and capability to raise voice against various issues.

8.1.1 Self-empowerment: One specific area for improving the effectiveness of women panchayat leaders is self-empowerment. The skills and abilities that need to be developed in the women leaders, to call them "empowered" have been identified below.

1. Self-confidence.
2. Ability to understand the public.
3. Ability to view public quality without discrimination.
4. Ability to march forward.
5. Ability to take decisions.
6. Ability to ensure public participation.
7. Ability to provide total literacy.
8. Financial independence.

8.1.2 Social Mobilization with Gender Focus: When we talk about gender focussed social mobilization, it includes alliances of women and for the women. But for social mobilisation, it is critical to have a mass of social capital. Thus, social capital and importance of alliance building for women PRI members cannot be ignored.

1. Willingness to do communal good.
2. Unity (amongst the members of the community).
3. Concern for community well-being.
4. Mutual trust.
5. System of participatory community decision-making.
6. Existence of social institutions.

There is a need for free flow of information to the women members of the panchayats, building a system by which the members of PRIs can exchange data and information, building the capability of the members of PRIs to build and sustain alliances to take forward issues of governance at local level (including tackling interference, building bridges with the bureaucracy and cutting out payment of bribes) and establishing a network of members of panchayats to lobby for changes and for advocacy.

To facilitate the capacity building of women members of

PRIs, training has to be imparted on philosophy, law, panchayati raj governance, structure, gender and the Indian Constitution which would be relevant to PRIs. Skills have to be developed in elements of planning for social and economic development and programme management at the village level. The women functionaries have to be trained in finding ways and means to offer effective challenge and resistance to invidious social mores, customs, beliefs and stereotyping that disempower women functionaries. These could be organizational, institutional or structural. Further, they also require guidance on building and sustaining mechanisms and systems to counter rampant public thievery of panchayat funds.

8.1.3 Training Programmes: Training programmes should ensure continuity and touch upon several aspects and not only on the basics of panchayati raj and knowledge about government schemes. The government training programmes lack a comprehensive and gender sensitive approach. The NGOs' training programmes are limited in terms of outreach and frequency, though strong on ideological front. Women face multiple oppressions and have to cope with additional problems of domestic responsibilities, travel expenses and patriarchal control on their mobility. The training package has to be more meaningful which imparts practical skills and encourages them to take on the political challenge.

Lack of empathy and support to PRIs by political and bureaucratic structures has created innumerable hurdles in the functioning of these agencies. Institutionalised inequalities and pressures sabotage attempts at capacity building of elected women representatives. It is important to create platforms that would act as pressure points to force powers that-be to bring about changes in attitudes and behaviour of political and bureaucratic executive towards women functionaries of PRIs .

Stressing the need for making these provisions truly effective, there is a critical necessity of empowering women and doing away with surrogate representatives for this purpose. "Training of women representatives must not begin with the promise that women are themselves responsible for the lack of social and cultural capital. The situation is a systematic failure. Therefore, even the trainer must start from what the participants know and then take them to the arena of the unknown...Building up community support networks for women members should be an important component of training intervention" (RGF Task Force Report, 2001).

Emphasis on procedures and programmes, rather than political process and critical issues that women encounter, is not going to usher in a qualitative change in the participation of women. Majority of women representatives are now showing their determination to occupy public space and are fighting for their rights and legitimate space. In their struggle against entrenched systems disempowering them, they have to overcome many hurdles, such as conditions of poverty, social responsibility for the domestic unit, growing criminalisation of political process and interlocking of other social relations with gender relations. This is just a small beginning, though, and much remains to be done before we can actually claim to have empowered the women elected members of panchayati raj.

Experience has taught people to go slow to approach their goals indirectly. They have to decide if attending panchayat meetings is sometimes worth missing their daily wage. This is even more so in the case of women, who have to worry about crying babies and hungry husbands. Thus, as of now, it is unrealistic to expect much in terms of their response. It has first to be demonstrated that the system is indeed here to stay.

8.2 PRIs and Traditional Institutions

The new system coexists with traditional institutions. The elders wield power in a way the Constitution may not have foreseen. If the PRIs are to succeed in their main goals, then they must work in harmony with these traditional institutions, not confront them head-on. This is easier said than done. The traditional institutions have not given space for women. Many of the factors that hindered women in the earlier system continue to exist and operate in rural areas. In fact, gender as a phenomenon hardly ever appears in a pure form. It is almost always alloyed with caste, class and religious factors. In matters where there is a clash between gender and caste or class, it is impossible to expect women to align themselves with other women, going against their caste or class loyalties. Some women have developed political ambitions too, especially when it is seen as a quick means for upward mobility. And political survival will be difficult if they betray class and caste interests. This is why the reservation of the post of president to the SC/ST category is so resented. The problem is in society, not in the panchayat that only reflects social reality.

The main problem that the women face in panchayati raj is per se in the exercise of the powers and function as a whole which have been provided by the Constitution to them. This is because of lack of delegation, resources and 'archaic' mindset of men in their home, in society and in the bureaucracy. The most important problem relates to the difficulties they are facing in the form of 'interference of Government officials and other influential persons in their jurisdiction'.

8.3 Problems/Challenges Faced by Women in Panchayats

An analysis of the challenges clearly reveals the structural, social and administrative issues. Changes in social mores and mindset of people at large are critical for women in PRIs to be effective. With archaic social mores and mindset, family support for women working in PRIs is hesitant at best and outright hostile at worst. This is a major issue that must be tackled.

On the structural issues, the challenge of increasing the representation of women in PRIs via the reservation route seems well entrenched. If the mass of women in PRIs increases to match the proportion of women in the total population, the number of women in PRIs will increase. With the increase in "mass" of women in PRIs, the quality of the performance of women in PRIs will also improve which in turn will lead to better governance at the local level. The challenge of increasing reservation of seats for women members from the existing 33 percent to 50 percent is formidable.

On the administrative issues, building "bridges", with the bureaucracy is a big challenge. With "restrained" devolution of resources and limited delegation of powers, the bureaucracy still holds the key to the success of women in PRIs. Starting from changing the bureaucrats' perception about women, their attitudes and behaviour towards panchayat functionaries, to their willingness to let go of their hold on the PRIs for the good of the greatest number, all make up a complex inter-locking challenge for the women in PRIs.

Some of the challenges are as under:

1. Proper support from Government officials is not forthcoming.
2. Political interference from other sources.
3. Social forestry is not entrusted to panchayats.
4. There is no official/formal relationship between self-help group (SHGs) and gram panchayats.
5. Securing 50 percent representation for women in PRIs.
6. Establishing rapport with government officials.
7. Arranging to provide knowledge about duties and roles of both female and male members of PRIs.
8. Increase transparency in the functioning of panchayats.
9. Forming *panchayat maitri* groups.
10. Demonstrating that women are "as good or better than men".
11. Raising funds.
12. Secretary is not accountable to gram panchayat.

If we look at the issue of political interference, the crux of the problem again boils down to non-delegation of powers and lack of ability of the women functionaries to resist interferences (from politicians, contractors, husbands and 'other sources'). The core-strategy to ward off external interference to the working of the PRIs would be to empower the women in panchayats and create a "body" of such women which can act as a source of support to them and as a pressure point against insidious interference by outsiders.

8.4 Village Level Planning

Developing a village level plan according to the demands of the community and implementation of the approved plans in the village are major roles of panchayat members. Starting from the preparation to the implementation of the plan, these representatives face a series of problems as given below.

The key issues relating to planning are paltry devolution of resources and public thievery. Because resources do not come to the gram panchayats, funds pass through bureaucratic channel which delays execution of works and more importantly, takes its slice of the cake. The seriousness of the "cuts" assumes even greater importance because, the resource base of PRIs being small, a cut makes it even smaller.

Women and challenges are almost synonymous terms. As the Indian society is not very open towards women, they face challenges both at the political and social levels. Most of the challenges faced by women functionaries in the PRIs in different states have a lot in common.

9

Women, Micro Finance and Self-help Groups (SHGs)

9.1 Meaning and Role of Micro Finance

Micro finance is a movement whose objective is a world in which as many poor and near-poor households as possible have permanent access to an appropriate range of high quality financial services, including not just credit but also savings, insurance, and fund transfers. Many of those who promote micro finance believe that such access will help poor people get out of poverty. For others, micro finance is a way to promote economic development, employment and growth through the support of micro entrepreneurs and small businesses.

Micro finance is a broad category of services, which includes micro credit. Micro credit is provision of credit services to poor clients. Micro credit is one of the aspects of micro finance and the two are often confused. Under micro credit, small amounts of loans are given to the borrower but under micro finance besides loans many other financial services are provided such as saving accounts, insurance etc. Therefore, micro finance is a wider concept as compared to micro credit.

The term *micro credit*, as a part of micro finance, did not exist before the 1970s. Now it has become a buzzword among the development practitioners. In the process, the term has been imputed to mean everything to everybody. No one now gets shocked if somebody uses the term micro credit to mean agricultural credit, or rural credit, or co-operative credit, or consumer credit, credit from the savings and loan associations, or from credit unions, or from money lenders.

There are currently a few social interventions that have

been combined with micro finance to increase awareness of HIV/AIDS, and gender equity. Such interventions educate on different gender roles, gender-based violence, and HIV/AIDS infections to strengthen the communication skills and leadership of women. Micro finance has also been combined with business education and with other packages of health interventions.

Micro finance programmes have been instrumental in generating employment, income and enhancing living standards of poor in underdeveloped and developing countries. They have good potential for uplifting the economic conditions of assetless poor people through group approach. Micro finance through self-help groups ensures active participation and involvement of the beneficiaries in effective implementation of the programmes for socio-economic development.

In India, micro finance programme has a crucial role to play in uplifting people living below poverty line. Poor people have less access to financial services because of their inability to provide collateral security which is demanded by the banks.

Micro finance is a form of financial services for entrepreneurs and small businesses lacking access to banking and related services. The two main mechanisms for the delivery of financial services to such clients are: (a) relationship-based banking for individual entrepreneurs and small businesses, and (b) group-based models, where several entrepreneurs come together to apply for loans and other services as a group. There is a rich variety of financial institutions in India which serve micro entrepreneurs and small businesses.

A significant proportion of the working population in many developing countries survives through involvement in the informal sector. By offering people a means to grow their small businesses to the point where many employ other people, micro finance has flow-on effects for local economies, decreasing unemployment and providing incomes for other poor families in the community.

With an increased income and therefore more money spent on items such as food, clothing and transport, micro finance clients become active participants in their local economies, also benefiting the providers of those products and services. By boosting local economies, micro finance benefits the developing world.

9.2 Why Should Micro Finance Focus on Women?

Micro finance experts generally agree that women should be the primary focus of service delivery. Evidence shows that they are less likely to default on their loans than men. Because operating margins become tighter on the smaller loans delivered, many MFIs consider the risk of lending to men to be too high.

Women are typically poorer than men and have fewer options for earning a livelihood to provide adequate food, housing and education for their children. They are also the *change agents* of the family. Women are more likely to invest their earnings into improving the lives of the families. By encouraging women to take charge of their futures, MFIs can impact families and whole communities.

In developing countries, more women are involved in the informal labour sector. Men are more likely to be employed in contract work as labourers or overseas workers. Women are often left to support their families or supplement their husband's income by using any skills they possess. With limited resources to start or expand a small business, micro finance is attractive to women who are prepared to work hard to give their children a brighter future.

Micro finance generally targets poor women because they have proven to be reliable credit risks and when they have the financial means, they invest that money back into their families, resulting in better health and education and stronger local economies.

Micro finance has become a catch word in financial sector of many economies. Micro finance programmes have been instrumental in generating employment, income and enhancing living standards of poor in underdeveloped and developing countries. Most vulnerable and disadvantaged groups in India have been excluded by the organized financial sector on the ground that they are not bankable. The very objective of financial inclusion is to make available financial products and services to the lower income groups in order to enable them to undertake entrepreneurial activities and come out of the grip of poverty.

Experience shows that economic growth of any economy is associated with a well-nourished organized inclusive financial system. Inclusion of the poorest of the poor and empowerment of those neglected and underprivileged must be the agenda of the government for healthy growth and equal distribution of fruits of development.

Women, if empowered by giving opportunities, can become good social workers, political leaders and successful entrepreneurs. However, the pace of women empowerment through micro finance is slow due to some constraints which urgently need to be rooted out.

9.3 Self-help Groups (SHGs)

A self-help group (SHG) is a small voluntary association of 10-20 poor people from the same socio-economic background who come together for the purpose of addressing their common socio-economic problems through self-help and mutual help. They collect small savings (thrift) on regular basis. Out of the pooled money, small interest bearing loans are given to the members and some amount is deposited with a bank regularly. The bank lends money for economic activities of the group without collateral security and at market rates. The savings of poor members are pooled resources saved with great difficulty. This hard-earned money is termed as *warm money.* The money obtained by the group from outsiders, i.e. banks or MFIs is termed as *cold money.*

Most self-help groups are located in India, though SHGs

can also be found in other countries, especially in South Asia and Southeast Asia.

Members make small regular contributions over a few months until there is enough capital with the group to begin lending. Funds may then be lent back to the members or to others in the village for any purpose. In India, many SHGs are *linked* to banks for the delivery of micro credit.

SHGs are started by non-governmental organizations (NGOs) that generally have broad anti-poverty agendas. SHGs are seen as instruments for a variety of goals including empowering women, developing leadership abilities among poor people, increasing school enrolments, and improving nutrition and the use of birth control. Financial intermediation is generally seen more as an entry point to these other goals, rather than as a primary objective.

Self-help groups (SHGs) have been instrumental in initiating micro entrepreneurial activities among those poor people who have been neglected so far and far away from the process of social as well economic development. Self-help Group-Bank Linkage Programme is responsible for developing banking habits among the poorest of the poor people.

The basic objective of self-help group is the upliftment of poor people by means of micro economic activities so that the members get job opportunities, sustainable income and some assets for generation of regular income. There is tremendous enthusiasm in formation of the groups but care is not taken for their proper growth and survival.

The most significant contribution of SHGs is that they have been instrumental in building up enough confidence among the poor people and now they are ready to participate in the process of development. Many of these have been running fair price shops very successfully. A sizable number of the groups are working as caterers for the State Government-sponsored Mid-Day Meal Scheme. It is noteworthy that a good number of the SHGs have been marketing successfully the products of domestic as well as multinational corporations in remote rural areas.

9.3.1 Structure of a SHG: A self-help group may be registered or unregistered. It typically comprises a group of micro entrepreneurs having homogenous social and economic backgrounds, all voluntarily coming together to save small sums of money regularly, and mutually agreeing to contribute to a common fund and to meet their emergency needs on the basis of mutual help. They pool their resources to become financially stable, taking loans from the money collected by that group and by making everybody in that group self-employed. The group members use collective wisdom and peer pressure to ensure proper end-use of credit and timely repayment. This system eliminates the need for collateral and is closely related to that of solidarity lending, widely used by micro finance institutions. To make the book-keeping simple enough to be handled by the members, flat interest rates are used for most loan calculations.

9.3.2 Alternative Models of Micro Finance/SHGs: India has adopted a multi-agency approach for the development of its micro finance programme. All the major credit institutions, *viz.* commercial banks, co-operative banks, RRBs along with non-governmental organisations (NGOs) have been associated with the micro finance programme. The role of the delivering agents and their interface has led to alternative models of micro finance.

Generally, the SHGs need self-help promoting institutions (SHPIs) to promote and nurture them. These SHPIs include various NGOs, banks, farmers' clubs, government agencies, self-employed individuals and federations of SHGs. However, some SHGs have also been formed without any assistance from such SHPIs. Three distinct linkage models of micro credit are currently being followed in India.

Under Model-I, banks themselves take up the work of forming and nurturing the groups, opening their saving accounts and providing them bank loans.

Under Model-II, SHGs are formed by NGOs and formal

agencies but are directly financed by banks.

Under Model-III, SHGs are financed by banks using NGOs and other agencies as financial intermediaries. In areas where formal banking system faces constraints, the NGOs are encouraged to approach suitable bank for bulk loan assistance.

9.3.3 Benefits of SHGs: There are many advantages of financing through SHGs: (a) an economically poor individual gains strength as part of a group, (b) financing through SHGs reduces transaction costs for both lenders and borrowers, (c) lenders have to handle only a single SHG account instead of a large number of small-sized individual accounts, and (d) borrowers, as part of a SHG, cut down expenses on travel (to and from the branch and other places) for completing paperwork and on the loss of workdays in canvassing for loans.

A self-help group benefits its members in a number of ways.

1. Members are benefited with regular saving habits.
2. Easy availability of micro credit.
3. Creation of productive assets.
4. Financial discipline.
5. Status as an economic person.
6. Unity, fraternity and co-operation.
7. Development of entrepreneurship and leadership.
8. Employment to self and others.
9. Joint action for education, health, drinking water, housing, rural roads, family welfare and planning, sanitation, village cleanliness etc.
10. Exposure to the schemes for development, awareness about environment protection, prevention of social evils such as alcoholism, dowry, child marriages.

9.4 Women Self-help Groups (WSHGs)

In India, a task force was set up in 1987 by the Central Government under the leadership of NABARD for undertaking a sample survey of existing self-help groups and preparing a plan for channelling savings and credit through SHGs of poorest of the poor with the help of banks, government organizations and NGOs. NABARD started a national level pilot project linking 500 SHGs to banks in the year 1992. The task force defined micro finance as provision of thrift, credit and other financial services and products of very small amounts to the poor in rural, semi-urban and urban areas, for enabling them to raise their income levels to improve their standards of living.

NABARD has been supporting SHG-Bank Linkage Programme since 1992 in order to uplift the poor through micro finance. Similarly, micro finance through women self-help groups has been instrumental in empowering women economically and socially.

In India, two broad approaches prevail in case of micro financing, viz. Self-Help Group–Bank Linkage and micro finance institutions. In the context of growing demand for micro finance by self-help groups, RBI made linkage of self-help groups with banks as a priority sector activity in 1996. The Government of India has been supporting the programme by making special budgetary provision for promotion of self-help groups since 1999.

Women in India, even after 70 years of Independence, are victims of socio-economic-cultural disadvantages. Women self-help groups have potential of bringing positive changes for strengthening women economically, socially and politically. So, there is need for promotion and nourishment of women self-help groups in India.

The emergence and rapid multiplication of SHGs based on micro credit is a phenomenon that is gaining increasing importance in the development scenario. SHGs are being viewed by governments and NGOs as a strategy for both women's empowerment as well as poverty reduction. SHGs are a conduit for routing a wide range of government-sponsored development messages and schemes. NGOs have increasingly been adopting SHGs as a strategy to bring women together, at a faster pace and larger scale than the collective building processes adopted by them earlier. A number of powerful players like MFIs, NGOs, corporations and donors—all of whom have a significant and growing interest in the SHG phenomenon which centres on poor women—have entered the arena. Credit is a right that poor women must have access to.

The experience of SHGs has shown that they have provided improved access to credit. Poor women are now perceived by the mainstream financial sector as creditworthy. Women have used savings and credit for needs such as those related to education and health, and in particular for crisis related needs. Participation in SHGs has meant opportunities related to mobility and a legitimate space in the public realm for leaders of SHGs.

In accordance with the announcement made by Finance Minister P. Chidambaram in the 2012-13 Budget, the Union Cabinet on May 7, 2013 approved the provision of interest subvention for women SHGs operating under the NRLM, ensuring that they shall avail loans up to ₹ 3 lakh at an interest rate of seven percent per annum. This will financially strengthen women self-help groups (WSHGs) across India.

Additionally, women SHGs that repay loans in time will enjoy an additional 3 percent subvention, thereby reducing the effective rate to 4 percent.

9.4.1 Problems and Challenges: Self-help groups have been instrumental in initiating micro entrepreneurial activities among those poor people who have been neglected so far and far away from the process of social as well economic development. Self-help Group-Bank Linkage Programme is responsible for developing banking habits among the poorest of the poor people.

The most significant contribution of SHGs is that they have been instrumental in building up enough confidence among the poor people and now they are ready to participate in the process of development. Many of these have been running fair price shops very successfully.

A sizable number of the groups are working as caterers for

the State Government-sponsored Mid-Day Meal Scheme. It is noteworthy that a good number of the SHGs have been marketing successfully the products of domestic as well as multinational corporations in remote rural areas. SHG-Bank Linkage Programme in India is the largest poverty alleviation programme in the world. However, the programme is not without difficulties and challenges. Some of these are mentioned below.

Notwithstanding all the positive achievements, the overall picture is uneven and raises following concerns related to gender justice and livelihoods:

1. Despite the increased access to credit, there continues to be several hurdles faced by women when they want to access credit from banks. These include huge amounts of paperwork and the fact that women are often pressurized by banks to recover loans made earlier to men in the village as an unwritten conditionality before loans are released to them.
2. It is increasingly being reported that SHG members have limited control over financial resources that they borrow despite being the conduit for access to such credit through their groups. The burden of repayment of such loans falls almost exclusively on the women. As SHGs are almost exclusively women-only, often women become proxy to husband's demands without the men taking up the responsibility for repayment or proper utilization of these loans.
3. Many of the micro enterprise activities undertaken have tended to be unviable. Low levels of credit absorption capacity, low skill base and low asset base have been challenges to the SHG movement, which are yet to be addressed. Moreover, lack of skills, experience and technical support services to promote livelihoods and build sustainable interventions among the intermediary organizations especially NGOs etc. does not enable sustainable livelihood options to be developed.

4. Access to credit as the focus of the micro credit programmes looses sight of the fundamental issues of access and control over common resources such as water, forests etc. which are the mainstay of occupations of a large number of the rural poor. The fundamental livelihood concerns related to the existing economic realities of poor women's lives remain largely unaddressed in the process.
5. Lack of support from family members discourage woman to join SHGs. In case of mix groups, male members do not extend support to female members. So, the essential objective of SHG programme is defeated.
6. Economic activities undertaken by the members are traditional. Obviously, the activities generate lower income. So, the micro finance movement is losing its main objective of empowering poor people.
7. Political affiliations of group members disturb group activities. Actually, the concept of self-help group is based on co-operation principles, i.e. equality, mutual help, democracy and thrift. It is observed that political leaders are taking interest in formation of SHGs to add to their vote bank. Political interference might have adverse impact on the progress of self-help group movement.

The basic objective of self-help group is upliftment of poor people by means of micro economic activities so that the members get job opportunities, sustainable income and some assets for generation of regular income. There is tremendous enthusiasm in formation of the groups but care is not taken for their proper growth and survival.

Banks are expected to promote and assist self-help groups by way of linking them with saving and credit facilities. As a part of policy measures, micro financing has been included in priority sector lending. However, the performance of the banks especially in rural areas is not up to the mark.

The formation of common-interest groups on the basis of co-operative principles has been a common practice in socio-economic spheres of India. On the same line, the formation of women self-help groups has a positive impact, as it is evident, on their socio-economic-political empowerment and creation of adequate space for their development.

Micro financing through self-help groups has proved to be a strategic measure for organizing women in groups and promoting savings habits to gain access to institutional credit for their socio-economic development and empowerment.

9.5 SHG-Bank Linkage Programme

This is the bank-led micro finance channel which was initiated by NABARD in 1992. Under the SHG model the members, usually women in villages, are encouraged to form groups of around 10-15. The members contribute their savings in the group periodically and from these savings, small loans are provided to the members. In the later period, these SHGs are provided with bank loans generally for income generation purpose. Members of the group meet periodically when the new savings come in, recovery of past loans are made from the members and also new loans are disbursed. This model has been very much successful in the past and with time it is becoming more popular. The SHGs are self-sustaining and once the group becomes stable, it starts working on its own with some support from NGOs and institutions like NABARD and SIDBI.

Many self-help groups, especially in India, under NABARD's SHG-Bank-Linkage Programme, borrow from banks once they have accumulated a base of their own capital and have established a track record of regular repayments.

This model has attracted attention as a possible way of delivering micro finance services to poor people that have been difficult to reach directly through banks or other institutions. By aggregating their individual savings into a single deposit, self-help groups minimize the bank's transaction costs and generate an attractive volume of deposits. Through self-help groups, the bank can serve small rural depositors while paying them a market rate of interest.

The SHG-Bank Linkage Programme since its beginning has been predominant in certain states, showing spatial preferences especially for the southern region–Andhra Pradesh, Tamil Nadu, Kerala and Karnataka.

9.5.1 Graduation of Mature SHGs into Micro Enterprises: The core needs of savings and credit for consumption and production of SHGs are being met by the banking system. These SHGs have not only availed loans, but have also availed loans more than once. It is being emphasised that members of the older SHGs would now be in a position to graduate into micro enterprises by taking up income generating activities. It is a difficult task to find viable micro enterprises for millions of poor households in rural areas. Though micro enterprises is not a panacea for the complex problem of chronic unemployment and poverty, yet their promotion is a viable and effective strategy for achieving significant gains in incomes and assets of poor and marginalised people.

However, in the absence of any specific hand-holding strategy to provide financial and non-financial services in an integrated manner, graduation of SHG members from micro finance to micro enterprises has not been smooth due to several obstacles. NABARD is, therefore, undertaking a pilot project in select districts, particularly for members of matured SHGs for promotion to the stage of micro enterprises. NGOs have been selected in each district for implementing the pilot projects.

10

Women in PRIs: Indian Experiences

There is a big difference between representation and participation. It is easier to legislate representation, but it is rather a complex and difficult task to create conditions for participation. The proper representation does not automatically lead to proper participation. It is important that they are in a position to influence decision-making and prepare and implement the schemes for economic development and social justice.

Results from a nationwide survey of women's participation in panchayats suggest that a majority of the EWRs report an enhancement in their personal effectiveness and image after being elected. They also report a reduction in household responsibilities. There are many instances of EWR of the panchayat taking a keen interest and playing a significant role in the workings of grassroots politics. It has often been observed that women prioritize those developmental needs that seem to be more pressing from their perspective. EWRs have initiated work on plans of bringing in piped water in the village and also to build schools as against infrastructural development favoured by men. There are number of success stories where EWR of the panchayats have taken the lead in making efforts for smokeless stoves, crèches, community halls, and have taken the initiative in family and matrimonial matters, counselling abusive and/or alcoholic husbands. Women are also seen to be more involved in monitoring the presence of teachers and medical staff in the school or health centre, and inspecting nutrition centres under the Integrated Child Development Scheme. Sometimes, women-headed panchayats have even experienced a dramatic increase in their revenues, sponsoring the auction of village ponds, community forests and village markets for the larger welfare of the community.

A study of Karnataka by Neema Kudva (2003) [1] reveals that in Karnataka, the reservation for women in panchayati raj institutions has seen mixed results: it has made women more visible, has decreased the level of corruption in panchayati raj institutions, and increased self-efficiency of women representatives. According to her, gender quota is a crucial component of strategies that seek to empower women through increased participation in the political system. However, it is difficult to claim that this formal participation has changed certain institutional practices and accountability.

All the women who participated in the election or also in the election process are getting empowered. Reservation has at least succeeded in bringing the womenfolk in rural India into the political forum and elected women could now imagine standing against a man in future. [2] This enormous expansion of women's representation in decentralized government structures has highlighted the advantages of proximity, namely the redress of grievance and most important of all the ability to mobilize struggle at a local level. For women themselves, there is an overwhelming sense of empowerment, of changed lives.

Devaki Jain (1996) [3] in her paper 'Panchayat Raj: Women Changing Governance', argues that reservations in panchayats has changed the governance system in India. She has pointed out that the enormous expansion of women's representation in decentralized government structures has highlighted the advantages of proximity, namely the redress of grievance and most important of all, the ability to mobilize struggle at a local level. She has presented a case study of Karnataka where she found that the number of women that panchayat reservation has brought into the political system has made a difference. By 1994, 330,000 women had entered politics as a result of reservation system and many more have been elected in the last two years. The percentage of women at various levels of political activity has shifted dramatically as a result of this Constitutional change, from 4-5 percent before panchayat raj institution (PRIs) to 25-40 percent after the PRIs. But the difference is also qualitative, because these women are bringing their experience in governance of civic society into governance of the State. In this way, they are making the State sensitive to issues of poverty, inequality and gender injustice.

Contrary to the above study, Shiv Kumar Lal (2007) in his paper, 'A Study of Issues and Challenges in Empowerment of Women through their Participation in the Panchayat Raj Institution: A Case Study of Allahabad District of Uttar Pradesh', [4] reveals that increased political participation of women in village panchayats did not had a significant bearing on women empowerment. His study also revealed that most of women elected representatives in panchayats had very minor role in decision-making mostly they are dummy. According to him, this is because of the lack of availability of forums and lack of proper grievance redressal mechanism for gender related issues.

Esther Duflo (2005) in her outstanding paper, 'Why Political Reservation', [5] critically examined whether political reservation is necessary for weaker sections of the society, as several countries including India have explicit quotas for disadvantaged groups to ensure their political representation. In the case of women, he pointed out that a large body of literature focusing on decision-making within the household has shown that women and men do different things and have different preferences. According to her, empirically women and men seem to have different policy preferences. For instance, she has mentioned about cases of West Bengal and Rajasthan. She found that women and men are concerned about very different types of public goods.

According to her, the potential beneficiaries of reservations have different political preferences than the majority and this would not in itself be sufficient to ensure that reservations have had any impact as long as candidates can commit to a policy platform in advance. Hence, he is very sceptical about the reservation as the very idea of political commitment leading to good governance. But he does recognize that reservation is necessary for the weaker sections if the elected representatives have to focus on the majority needs. To summarize, he stated that in the case of women, it is seen that women policymakers provide goods whose quality and quantity match that of men, and they appear to be less likely to ask for bribes in return. Despite this, villagers are less satisfied with the performance of female leaders than with the performance of male leaders.

Non-governmental organizations (NGOs) have been supporting women representatives in different aspects like education, training programmes etc. to sustain their participation.

These NGO networks are working as civil society space for public action. Amitabh Behar and Yamini Aiyar (2003), [6] found that the growing success of networks of elected women representatives clearly demonstrates the significance of micro initiatives in institutionalizing the panchayati raj system. The civil society networks are working for the capacity building for the women elected representatives in political arena particularly with a view to contribute to the growing debate on finding alternatives, bottom-up strategies for strengthening institutions of local self-governance and facilitating the formation of effective associations of local self-governments. According to author, experiences of the networking strategy is crucial not only for the impact it has on strengthening local self-government in India but also for its potential to provide noteworthy insights for civil society actors in particular and the civil society discourse in the country in general.

Most of these networks have been initiated as innovative capacity building strategies for elected women representatives. In practice, these initiatives have gone beyond their primary mandate and entered the political arena by using these networks to engage in advocacy and negotiations with the state. In some cases, the networks have, directly entered the political mainstream and have developed as recruitment grounds for political parties. Therefore, in this context, it remains important to note that the facilitating non-governmental organizations have a crucial role to play in bringing elected women representatives together, mobilizing them to form networks and providing relevant support to the networks on a need basis. However, the strategy of forming networks of EWRs has been useful but till now has been unable to take a decisive shift into the next phase, where these networks are clearly articulated as political formations and not merely as capacity building exercises.

Importantly, the initiators have to view this strategy as operating in the political domain and provide support to interventions that are not merely limited to core tasks of association formation and capacity building but to prepare the ground for the networks of EWRs to take political action. To conclude, it can be considered that these networks need to be viewed as an important step in the direction of strengthening democracy in the country.

The NGOs and civil society organizations are working with women representatives and building networks, which is helping women representative in their decision-making process in day to day political affairs. But the deficiencies which persist in all the three levels of panchayti raj system, many a time, creates problem in the working of panchyati raj institutions (PRIs). Aureliano Fernandes (2003), [7] in his paper stated that deficiencies in facilitating the potential of panchayati raj persist at three levels—state, panchayati raj institutions and societal levels. Government at the state level with a patrimonial perception of self and aggrandizer instincts has pushed the 'self-governance participatory model' of the panchayats to the periphery, both at the level of discourse and praxis. This coupled with conceptual inadequacies, epistemic and operational constraints, poor finances, and political interference have posed a serious challenge to the realization of the potential role envisaged for panchayats in the 73rd Amendment. He suggested that if panchayati raj has to fulfil its foundational tenets of empowering the community, there is a need to recognize the primacy of societal good over individual or political goals. PRIs have to transform themselves into community institutions fulfilling a social contract with an all inclusive participatory planning and associationalism as essential methodologies.

Finally, he has suggested some strategies for the devolution of powers to PRIs but he has also strongly stated that the form of governance envisioned by panchayati raj, which is egalitarian, participatory and all-inclusive catering to the needs of village communities cannot emerge by strategies alone. Strategies would be successful to the extent that they enhance the dawning of the 'age of reason', a sort of a 'political enlightenment' or the political class, where they arrive at a realization that long-term societal goals have a primacy over individual or short-term political goals.

In another study J.S. Sodhi and M.S. Ramanujam (2006), [8] discussed panchayti raj from a historical point of view and emphasized on the point that all the categories of women beneficiaries (SC/ST/OBC) are given preferential treatment. According to the authors, there are provisions for reservations for women. However, such reservations for SC and ST women do not appear to have brought about a culture of effective participation in the panchyati raj system (PRS) due to a variety of reasons such as illiteracy and poverty. Besides, the difficulty of such persons to change their age-old customs and practices is also an important reason for their being not effective in delivering development. He suggested that as women are one of the neglected categories, there should be a separate quorum for attendance of women and for attendance at gram sabha meetings and there must be special training for women at the gram sabha level.

In addition to that, each village should have a mahila mandal and SC/ST/OBC persons should be encouraged to form self-help groups (SHGs). These bodies should be used to deliberate upon development needs of the village and the implementation of the development schemes approved. They should then decide the modalities of expressing the views of the weaker sections of the society in the gram sabha meetings. Further, authors emphasized the point that political parties and social activists should be encouraged to create greater awareness among the women about the importance of PRS and the need for active participation in gram sabha meetings.

In an excellent paper, Mani Shankar Aiyar (2002), [9] argued that economic reforms in India will not be effective if we put panchyati raj as a side show. According to him, panchayati raj needs to be made the fulcrum of the reforms process and economic reforms should integrate with planning and implementation through institutions of self-government, which will lead to grassroots empowerment and then grassroots development. Further, he noted that there is a special need to concentrate on training for the weaker sections and women. Some of the institutions have taken up the challenge of effectively training elected members and staff, especially representatives of the weaker sections and women, in the arts of panchayati raj.

In view of the crucial importance of adequate women's participation in meetings of the gram sabha, a sub-quorum of female attendance should be built into the required quorum. Moreover, provision may be made that meetings of the gram sabha be preceded by meetings of the mahila sabha, comprising all adult women voters of the village panchayat, to ensure that gender concerns and preferences get fully reflected in the proceedings of the gram sabha. Finally, he emphasized the point to involve women in the planning process; consultation with the village-level mahila sabha should be built into the planning process.

As far as planning process is concerned, rural women are always out of decision-making. It is because women in rural communities are handicapped by caste, class and gender hierarchies, ethnic and religious discrimination as well as unequal distribution of resources. The paper by Kuntala Lahiri Dutt and Samanta Gopa (2002), [10] discusses some of the lacuna in government sponsored schemes with specific reference to women. From their field work, they found that the primary reason for the lack of performances of government schemes is because they are devised at the top by some urban based experts. Furthermore, women voices are rarely heard. The problem with self-help scheme is the way they problematize the 'self' mostly in the module of bureaucrat's own image rather than the real women. Thus, many a times, women are not decision makers and are not able to play a significant role in devising projects suitable to their needs as they should ideally do. So far as the PRIs are concerned, the same type of things can be seen in several places.

The essay by Bandyopadhyay and others (2003), analyzed historically, the roots of the basic contradictions which have haunted the rural self-governing institutions of India. According to him, these contradictions have been further sharpened by the Seventy-third constitutional amendment. Though the concept of self-government at the local level has been guaranteed by the Constitution, it has been given a go by in practice by the ruling establishments. Institutional changes brought about by the Seventy-third amendment have helped create a space at the grassroots level for these contradictions to be challenged by the disadvantaged sections. In the case of women, he pointed out that due to the Seventy-third Amendment, over a million women have come out of their homes for the first time in centuries to hold public office and to participate in public activities. This has been the most effective formal step towards political empowerment of women.

There are, of course, stories about how women representatives have been manipulated by the male folks in the family, or by the political parties and power groups, but there are also numerous instances of women exercising political power thereby enhancing their standing both in the society and in the family against heavy odds. Through this, it is not only those who get elected are getting empowered formally and substantively but all the women who participated in the election or in the election process are also getting empowered.

However, some scholars like Mohanty (1995), [11] questioned the empowerment of the women as the reservations did not actually empower the community. According to her, if reservations for women in panchayati raj institutions are to lead to their empowerment in real terms, social, economic and political conditions which facilitate and encourage their participation, need to be created. She mentioned about the history of PRIs from Seventy-third Amendment and discussed about some specific states like Orissa and Rajasthan. She also talked about factors affecting women's empowerment. She has rightly pointed out the social hierarchies in Indian society and where women by and large not decision-makers. Their 'decisions' in most cases have been influenced by the wishes and dictates of the male family members. They are guided by a patriarchal social system and, therefore, are discriminated against in terms of access to food and health care.

Another important aspect which affect women's empowerment is their economic independence. According to her, even administrators do not also take much interest in the specific problems of women. Finally, she mentioned that for all these reasons, women should be made aware of the deficiencies of the bureaucracy and the bureaucrats should be made more sensitive to the needs of women. In sum, women have to cross many hurdles before becoming effective partners in the decision-making process.

Ramaswamy in her excellent easy on 'India's Crisis of Governance: The Women's Perspective' (2005), [12] pointed out that India is a practicing democracy and is one of its major achievements. But one must not be oblivious to the incompleteness of this democratic enterprise of the country, as women who constitute nearly half of the population occupy less than 10 percent of the Parliamentary seats. As a transitional major, a Constitutional amendment for reserving seats for women in municipal councils and panchayats was done by the Seventy-third and Seventy-fourth Amendments in 1992. However, in this, women find token representation in the political sphere and that the public domain, though not exclusively a male preserve, is surely dominated by men.

This proves that empowering women continues to be an elusive problem. According to her, there are two sides to the maleness of politics. At one level, there is the traditional patriarchal notion where politics is in the nature of a patron-client relationship paralleling the father-son relationship. As a result of this, women are excluded from the material benefits that politics accrues and even if they inherit the political office, it is usually due to the absence of a male member. The other male aspect of politics is fraternalism. In this essay, the author criticized all the political parties and state who are proponents of women reservation but they do not work for it even within their party level. She suggested that unlike in Scandinavian countries, to bring a feminine prospective in decision-making process, there are two important requirements that have to be attempted.

First, political parties and its affiliated organizations ought to re-invent themselves and become more sensitive and responsive to women. They should not use the quota law to appoint token women with little or no power; especially in bodies that do not have real decision-making powers. Second, there is the need to re-orient the socialization process by making equality the cornerstone of both societal and political culture.

In the past decade, good governance and decentralization have become two of the main development pillars in the quest for successful development. In India, steps have been taken to increase the participation of the weaker sections of the society in new arrangements for decentralized local decision-making through rules of reservation. Erik Bryld (2001), [13] in his work, discloses the potential and the pitfalls of increasing participation through decentralization by analyzing the Indian panchayati raj system from the field (Karnataka). It is shown how technocratic regulations are not sufficient to ensure genuine empowerment for all in democratic decision-making. For a successful development, empowerment of the weaker sections (SCs/STs/OBCs/women) of society is needed in order to lessen the inequalities.

All these different parts of society must be brought to participate in the decision-making processes, if democracy is to offer something for everyone. The study conducted a field work in the Kolar district of Karnataka state and data reveals that generally the experiences from India have been very good compared to other developing countries. The overall satisfaction with the system and the participatory level has been very impressive, but it seems to have had little effect on the weaker sections of society. The field work also revealed that the majority of women's life forms around the private sphere while the majority of men's life forms around the public sphere.

Reservation brings women into the panchayat office but cannot really be said to empower rural Indian women due several factors like illiteracy, language barriers, inexperience or low respect among fellow villagers which are some of the main problems besetting active participation in the decision-making of the majority of panchayat members elected under reservation. Especially, many female panchayat members lack basic capabilities for working within this system. Their illiteracy, inexperience, and language barriers mean that they are not actively participating in the work of the panchayat and are often ignored by male counterparts. Decentralization has not resulted in empowerment for these women.

The study by Jana Everett (2009), [14] in Pune district of Maharashtra on elected women representatives (EWRs) of PRIs shows that in some cases, the will to empower is hijacked by lower-level government officials, dominant groups, and men and women are not incorporated into local politics. In other cases, the will to empower reaches rural women, instilling in them a desire to participate and increased capacities to do so. Finally, she concluded that that the emphasis of a strong Foucauldian perspective on structure at the expense of agency obscures the complexity of women's responses. In contrast, a weak Foucauldian perspective is able to recognize that in some cases these incorporation processes create assertive, reformist, and resourceful citizens.

Democratic local governance, now a major sub-theme within the overall context of democratic development, promises that government at the local level can become more responsive to citizen's desires and more effective in service delivery. Based on a six country study, the author Harry Blair (2000), [15] argued that there is a significant potential for promoting local governments but there are some limitations in two things—participation and accountability. In the case of India, he pointed out that although India has conducted elections periodically since panchyati raj was introduced but intimidation and vote buying happens more often than other countries under the study. In the case of accountability, there are scopes with serious constraints. Finally, the author suggested that there is considerable scope for enhancing both participation and accountability at the local level. On the participation side, local government can bring new elements, particularly women and minorities, into local politics in meaningful ways. They can gain representation in local decision-making and, where some degree of geographical concentration exists, empowerment as well.

While talking about empowerment, participation and decision-making etc. we always encountered one problem that is corruption. Earlier, we have also talked about vote buying as an aspect of bad representation but here Sten Widmalm (2005), [16] pointed out one of major challenges in the local self-government; that is corruption. This study of decentralization reforms in India challenges the assumption that corruption should be seen as a function of culture. Data analysis in the study shows that in the individual level support for a modernized or humanized version of the Weberian bureaucratic model and the position against bribes is strong but at the village level it is not so strong. But the data also shows that intra-group trusts are important, providing counterweight to corruption. So it can be said that at an aggregate level, social capital plays an important role for resisting corruption.

Another study on the women participation in the politics in local self-government and corruption by Vijayalakshmi (2008), reveals that although nearly 40 percent of the elective positions in the institutions of local government are occupied by women; there is no significant gender difference in attitudes towards rent-seeking or in actual levels of corruption between male and female representatives. The study examines the relationship between corruption and gender in the context of local government in India, using a Logit model to investigate the assumption that women's participation in electoral politics suggests that the presence of more women in government will engender public policy, and also tends to reduce corruption. But the evidence as said earlier shows that gender is not a significant factor in explaining levels of corruption. The results also suggest that institutional measures such as accountability, risk factor and the role of opposition parties were crucial in explaining the level of corruption. To consider gender as a factor in corruption has several limitations, unless it is seen in conjunction with the status of women in different areas of political space.

As we have discussed above some of obstacles of female participation in the politics, 'Female Political Participation and Health in India' (2001) is an important easy by Suzanneg Leason which has discussed about different determinants of female political participation using a unique data set. She has studied the relation between health, literacy and income of women with the political participation. The study found that literacy and income have the anticipated effects for voting. But regarding health outcomes, the results have been disappointing. As far as health indicator is concerned, she found that there is no impact on female participation on child survival.

As we see the evolution of women's representation in panchayats, women's representation and presence has continued to be influenced by the same ideology and tokenism as has continued at other political levels despite the political equality guaranteed by the Constitution. However, the 1992 Amendment has given a new direction for their representation in panchayats by guaranteeing a critical base of one-third representation which has not been possible so far in other political institutions whether the legislature or the party organizations despite pronouncements by almost all the political parties to the contrary (Buch, 2000). [17] Buch (2000), found that the experience of women, their representation, participation, and their impact on the socio-political context are quite encouraging. There is a general conception that "women have come into politics as proxy candidates and continue to be manipulated by powerful patriarchal elites".

However, the study found that the work of a women chairperson of a panchayat in tribal district of Jhabua of Madhya Pradesh is amazing. Her leadership, command, confidence and clarity in dealing with the school teachers and panchayat secretary is amazing. The above example may not be sufficient to generalize but it can be said that reservations have provided an opportunity for women's entry into a non-traditional space and a possibility for erosion of traditional gender, caste and class roles and hierarchy.

Another very systematic study on the participation of women in political sphere shows a strong argument that a more equal gender representation will increase policy congruence (Lindgren et al., 2009). This article has examined the hotly debated question of whether increasing the representation of women in important decision-making positions in society could be an effective means of obtaining a better match between the political preferences of the elite and those of the masses. The results from the empirical analysis—using data on nearly 5,000 elite-mass dyads within 24 Indian villages—are indeed challenging because they show that women are not only better equipped than men to politically represent women but also that they are better at representing men—and the results are shown to apply in highly different socio-economic contexts.

A study by Shaibal Gupta (2001), [18] in Bihar shows that 2001 panchayat elections can be seen as the decisive emergence of the lower backward castes. Their presence in the power structure as *mukhia* and *zilla parishad* chairmen indicates that new social and political equations are emerging at the local level. The panchyat elections of 2001 were held in Bihar after a lapse of 23 years and the data shows Bihar as a turning point for the electoral empowerment of the lower backwards. Till recently, they were not given political or social importance although they constituted more than 33 percent of the total population. These elections have revealed that they are no longer an electoral fodder for the upper backwards.

The participation or representation we have discussed above is all because of the women's movement in the country. But specifically, rural women's movement is not very successful in our country. Madhu Kishwar (1988), [19] in her paper discussed about the limits of rural women participation in women movements. According to her, there are five most important factors which limits their participation. Firstly, rural women in most parts of India have no independent means of support and little control over family income even when they make major contributions to it. They are typically dependent on men of the family for sustenance and therefore for approval of any activity they undertake. In such a situation, it is difficult to develop a sense of group identity with other women, as separate and distinct from identification with the family unit. Secondly, women in most parts of India, particularly in north,

north-west and central India are not allowed to develop alliances outside the family.

Alliances with men are prevented as being liable to be compromised with a woman's and the family's reputation, while alliances with women are also discouraged unless they are part of larger family alliances. Thirdly, it is a simple fact that most rural women are so heavily over worked that they have next to no time and energy to put into building a movement except when men, in the interests of a larger community-based struggle, decide to relieve the women of some household responsibilities and free them to join in specific and limited movement activities. Fourthly, most rural women are deprived of elementary skills required to keep a movement alive, such as literacy, numeracy and information about and exposure to the world outside. Lastly, because of these reasons, few rural women choose to work full time for a movement or an organization.

Madhu Kishwar (1996), in her another important work on women and politics, discussed about the women's role in politics and that it should not be the only basis for reservation. It should be more than that. She has rightly pointed out that "we need wide spectrum electoral reforms that will curb the role of muscle and money power in politics and democratize decision-making in the political parties and a sensible proportional representation system which facilitates representation of various marginalized groups without mechanical reservation quotas". She has also mentioned some corrective measures for the political participation of women beyond the reservation system.

We have discussed above about the participation of women in the political sphere and found successes and failures of the same in different parts of the country. The article by Kaushik and Shaktawat (2010) is an addition to the studies we have reviewed about the question of women's competence in active politics. [20] This is an empirical study of the situation at the ground level in Chittorgarh district of Rajasthan. This study was conducted by employing questionnaires, interviews, and observation methods in December 2005, which included 14 women zila parishad (district council) members and the woman *zila pramukh* (chairperson) of the district.

The study shows that there are 35 members in the district council; out of these, 14 members and the *zila pramukh* are women elected on the seats reserved for women as per the Seventy-third Amendment Act. The study found that women's effective participation in the panchayati raj or the latter's usefulness for women's rights and development will become a reality only if panchayat system itself operates in a principled, democratic, and meaningful way. Hence, the need of the hour is to strengthen the system and involve greater people's participation. Moreover, there is need for women to be politically mobilized for contesting elections and even campaigning and questioning the candidates. For women who are already in the PRIs, literacy and political education programs are needed.

A number of papers have already examined the issue, in different settings, about the political reservation for disadvantaged groups and is believed to be a way of improving targeting of publicly provided goods to these groups. The paper by Pranab Bardhan et al. (2010), studies the effect of political reservations in local governments in favour of women, scheduled castes and scheduled tribes (SCs/STs) in the Indian state of West Bengal regards the provision of government services and local public goods. This paper examines the impact of political reservations for women and scheduled caste and scheduled tribe (SC/ST) candidates in local governments in West Bengal in India between 1998 and 2004.

The study found that, in regard to effect of women reservations, there is no improvement in any dimension of targeting; rather a worsening of intra-village targeting of SC/ST groups. In contrast, it found that a significant positive effect of SC/ST *pradhan* reservation on per capita benefits in the village as a whole, and on intra-village targeting of female headed households, as well as the group (SC or ST) for whom the position is reserved. The improvements in village-level benefits partially redressed a systematic tendency for higher level governments to allocate lower benefits to villages with high SC/ST population. Joint reservations of *pradhan* position for women SC/ST candidates resulted in a mixture of the respective effects of reservations for women and SCs/STs—an improvement in village average benefits, and deterioration in a number of dimensions of intra-village targeting.

From the above discussion, we can say that yet there is a little consensus on the appropriate way to develop governance structures that are responsive to the interests of the poor. These remain unclear because the impact of representation is not uniform as far as the distribution of public goods is concerned. The paper entitled, "The Politics of Public Good Provision: Evidence from Indian Local Governments" (2004), takes a preliminary look at the resource allocation by elected village governments using data from three Indian states. The study suggests that overall, relative to *non-pradhan* villages; the *pradhan's* village will be allocated more public goods. The difference in allocation will, however, vary by type of public goods. It also found that the effects of *pradhan's* group identity on policy, the agenda setting powers of the *pradhan* and the extent of spillovers associated with different types of public goods (Timothy and Pande et al., 2004).

Endnotes

1. Kudva, Neema (2003), "Towards Gender Equity: Policies and Strategies", *International Journal of Politics, Culture, and Society,* Vol. 16, No. 3, Spring, pp. 445-463.
2. Bandyopadhyay, D., Saila K. Ghosh and Buddhadeb Ghosh (2003), "Dependency Versus Autonomy: Identity Crisis of India's Panchayats", *Economic and Political Weekly,* Vol. 38, No. 38, September 20-26, pp. 3984-3991.
3. Jain, Devaki (1996), "Panchayat Raj: Women Changing Governance", September, Gender in Development, Monograph

Series #5, UNDP, New York.

4. Lal, Shiv Kumar (2007), "A Study of Issues and Challenges in Empowerment of Women through Their Participation in the Panchayat Raj Institution: A Case Study of Allahabad District of Uttar Pradesh".
5. Duflo, Esther (2005), "Why Political Reservations?", *Journal of the European Economic Association*, Vol. 3, No. 2/3, Papers and Proceedings of the Nineteenth Annual Congress of the European Economic Association, pp. 668-678.
6. Behar, Amitabh and Yamini Aiyar (2003), "Networks of Panchayat Women: Civil Society Space for Political Action", *Economic and Political Weekly*, Vol. 38, No. 47, pp. 4936-4940.
7. Fernandes, Aureliano (2003), "Government and Local Governance", *Economic and Political Weekly*, Vol. 38, No. 27, July, pp. 2873-2879.
8. Sodhi, J.S. and M.S. Ramanujam (2006), "Panchayati Raj System: A Study in Five States of India", *Indian Journal of Industrial Relations*, Vol. 42, No. 1, pp. 1-41.
9. Aiyar, Mani Shankar (2002), "Panchayati Raj: The Way Forward", *Economic and Political Weekly*, Vol. 37, No. 31, pp. 3293-3297.
10. Dutt, Kuntala and Gopa Lahiri (2002), "State Initiatives for the Empowerment of Women of Rural Communities: Experiences from Eastern India", *Community Development Journal*, Vol. 6, No. 2, pp. 137-156.
11. Mohanty, Bidyut (1995), "Panchayati Raj: 73rd Constitutional Amendment and Women", *Economic and Political Weekly*, Vol. 30, No. 52, December, pp. 3346-3350.
12. Ramaswamy, Sushila (2005), "India's Crisis of Governance: The Women's Perspective", *Policy and Society*, Vol. 24, Issue 3, pp. 122-141.
13. Bryld, E. (2001), "Increasing Participation in Democratic Institutions through Decentralization: Empowering Women and Scheduled Castes and Tribes through Panchayat Raj in Rural India", *Democratization*, Vol. 8, No. 3, pp. 149-172.
14. Everett, Jana (2009), "Governance Reforms and Rural Women in India: What Types of Women Citizens Are Produced by the Will to Empower?", *Social Politics*, Vol. 16, Issue 2, pp. 279-302.
15. Blair, Harry (2000), "Participation and Accountability at the

Periphery: Democratic Local Governance in Six Countries", *World Development*, Vol. 28, No. 1, pp. 21-39.

16. Widmalm, Sten (2005), "Explaining Corruption at the Village and Individual Level in India: Findings from a Study of the Panchayati Raj Reforms", *Asian Survey*, Vol. 45, No. 5, pp. 756-776.
17. Buch, Nirmala (2000), "Women's Experience in New Panchayats: The Emerging Leadership of Rural Women", Occasional Paper No. 35, Centre for Women Development Studies, available at: http://www.cwds.ac.in/occasionalpapers.htm, retrieved on January 128, 2011.
18. Gupta, Shaibal (2001), "New Panchayats and Subaltern Resurgence", *Economic and Political Weekly*, Vol. 36, No. 29, pp. 2742-2744.
19. Kishwar, Madhu (1988), "Nature of Women's Mobilization in Rural India: An Exploratory Essay", *Economic and Political Weekly*, Vol. 23, No. 52/53, pp. 2754-2763.
20. Kaushik, Anupma and Gayatri Shaktawat (2010), "Women in Panchayati Raj Institutions: A Case Study of Chittorgarh District Council", *Journal of Developing Societies*, Vol. 26, No. 4, pp. 473-483.

11

Women in PRIs: A Case Study of Bihar

11.1 Bihar: An Introduction

Bihar has been the first state in the country to bring in 50 percent reservation for women in PRIs. This was made operational through Bihar Panchayat Raj Adhiniyam, 2006. Reservations of all categories would be under 50 percent. The scheduled caste and scheduled tribe reservation would be in proportion to their population. In all, maximum 20 percent reservations would be provided to the backward classes. In all categories, up to 50 percent reservation would be provided for women candidates. Same pattern and norms, as above, would be followed for the reservation for the posts of chairpersons; these would be on the basis of rotation.

Bihar is one of the backward states in the country with respect to human development indices like literacy, life expectancy and so on. Bihar has 9 divisions, 38 districts, 101 sub-divisions, 534 blocks and 45,102 revenue villages grouped into 8,463 gram panchayats. The panchayati raj institutions at district, block and village level are zilla parishads, panchayat samitis and gram panchayats respectively. Bihar also has gram katchahries at the gram panchayat level. There are 1,15,876 ward members.

With a sex ratio of 919, the gender gap in Bihar encompasses various dimensions of discrimination, marginalization and oppression. The gender gap is indeed in-built into gender relations which need to be addressed for balanced social development. The interventions by the state government to address gender disparity can be clubbed under following main heads:

1. Balika Cycle and Poshak Yojana to promote female education.

2. Kanya Suraksha Yojana to stop female foeticide.
3. Kanya Vivah Yojana.
4. Nari Shakti Yojana.

The state government has been publishing its gender budget since 2008-09.

This study adopts a combination of various research techniques. The methodology chosen follows a two-pronged strategy, including quantitative and qualitative approach. This is done with a view to producing a richer set of findings. The quantitative survey has been conducted to obtain precise and mostly pre-coded responses from each respondent individually. The structured schedules have been used in the survey which offers many benefits, e.g. biases have been controlled and probable errors reduced. On the other hand, the qualitative method has generated information that has been used to support the quantitative findings.

11.2 Schedules for Interview

The following schedules were devised for the quantitative survey:

1. Schedule for *adhyaksh*.
2. Schedule for *mukhiyas*/Ward Members.
3. Schedule for panchayat secretary.
4. Schedule for community/household.

In all, 31 female adhyakshs, 40 mukhiyas, 100 ward members, and 40 panchayat secretaries were covered across Bihar. The total number of community members (including both household and group/committee members) covered during the field survey was 400. The objective of the household interview was to triangulate the information gathered from the mukhiya and elected male and female representatives.

11.3 Qualitative Survey

For the qualitative survey, focus group discussions (FGDs) were conducted with the community, as well as in-depth interviews with Government officials and reviews of the minutes of meetings (MoM) of gram sabhas.

The guidelines/semi-structure schedules devised for the qualitative survey were the following:

1. FGD with community.
2. In-depth discussions with government officials.
3. Review of MoM.

The qualitative method generated information that was used to support the quantitative findings.

In all, 8 gram panchayats were selected within 8 districts on a random basis for the FGD. Out of 8 gram panchayats, 6 were female-headed and 2 were male-headed.

11.4 Rationale for Selecting the Districts for Study

The study adopted the method of random stratified sample, representing 6 divisions of Bihar, i.e. Tirhut division (Muzaffarpur, Sitamarhi, Sheohar, East Champaran), Darbhanga division (Samastipur), Patna division (Patna,) Purnea division (Purnea, Katihar), Kosi division (Suapul) and Magadh (Nawada).

Bihar suffers from considerable economic disparity across the districts. We considered district-wise gross domestic district product (GDDP) of 2006-07 at 1999-2000 prices. Economically prosperous district were Patna and Muzaffarpur. On the lower side were districts like Sitamarhi, Nawada, Purnea and Supaul.

More than 90 percent of the population in 25 out of 38 districts of Bihar lives in rural areas, making the state the least urbanised. The districts which we have chosen have more than 90 percent of population living in rural area except Patna which has 58.4 percent of the population in rural area.

11.5 Findings of the Study

11.5.1 Socio-Demographic and Economic Profile of Elected Women Representatives:

1. The educational attainment level of mukhiya was found to be higher (75.5 percent) than ward member (62.4 percent).

It was found that the mukhiyas had attained a higher level of education. Generally, educational attainment was up to middle-school or above among the elected representatives

2. The data on age reflects that the mukhiyas were normally of middle age compared to ward members who were younger than mukhiyas.
3. As regards the zilla parishad chairpersons, 61.53 percent belonged to young age, 23.07 belonged to middle age and the remaining 15.38 percent belonged to old age.
4. Distribution of elected representatives by caste reflects that a large portion of women mukhiyas belonged to disadvantaged groups (SC: 40.50 percent and BC: 40.64 percent). About 28 percent belong to the general category.
5. Out of the zilla parishad chairperson, 69.29 percent belonged to the reserved category and 30.73 percent belonged to the general category.
6. The mukhiyas had a better economic background, assessed according to the APL/BPL status.
7. 93.2 percent of the EWRs were first timers.
8. 65.5 percent of female ward members belonged to the BPL category where as 56.7 percent of the male ward members were BPL.
9. 29.3 percent of the women ward members were illiterate.
10. 65.5 percent of female ward members belonged to the BPL category whereas 56.7 percent of the male ward members were BPL.
11. Prior association with any form of politics was low. In most cases (85 percent), the act of contesting the first election signalled their entry into active politics.
12. Reservation emerged as an important motivator (49 percent) for contesting the first election as much as its withdrawal was an important reason for not contesting elections among the former women representatives (35 percent).
13. Husbands (35 percent) and other family members (15 percent) were reported as playing an important role in

motivating women representatives to contest elections for the first time. By contrast, their male counterparts were usually self-motivated (50 percent).

14. Elected women representatives (85 percent) were functioning within an enabling environment at the level of the village community and the household.
15. A supportive professional environment evidently motivated elected women representatives to perform better, as 65 percent reported an increase in their interaction with line departments and parallel bodies. Even the participation of common women citizens in various activities such as attending gram sabha meeting etc. had reportedly increased (68-78 percent).
16. Higher level of political aspiration was generally not present among gram panchayat level EWR representatives (85 percent). 85 percent did not contest any intermediate/zilla parishad elections. This aspiration was very high among the male members (91 percent).
17. 45 percent of EWRs did not receive formal training on rules and regulations of the panchayats for effective performance of their roles. 65 percent claimed that training was not held and 25 percent claimed that they were never called for it.
18. The data on age reflects that the mukhiyas were normally of middle age compared to ward members who were younger than the mukhiyas. Among the zilla parishad chairperson, 61.53 percent belonged to young age, 23.07 belonged to middle age and the rest 15.38 percent belonged to the old age.
19. Distribution of elected representatives by caste reflected that a large portion of women mukhiyas belonged to the disadvantaged groups (SC: 40.50 percent and BC: 40.64 percent). About 28 percent belonged to the general category. Among the zilla parishad chairpersons, 69.29 percent belonged to the reserved category and 30.73 belonged to the general category.

20. The greater part of the time of mukhiyas was spent in panchayat related work. Besides this, they were involved in farming and household work.

11.5.2 Study of Zila Parishad Chairpersons (26, all females): This is the preliminary finding from a 2011 survey. 26 chairpersons of zila parishad were interviewed. 34.6 percent belonged to the general category, 26.9 percent were to SCs and 19.2 percent belonged to the OBC category.

All said that they get support from community-based organizations and women groups. All of them opined that they got support from the spouse and their family members. 92.3 percent said that they had an enabling environment.

96.2 percent said that they required the permission to go out from the household. 80.8 percent opined that they did not have the voice in selection of grooms, but 88.5 percent expressed that they had a say in family planning.

11.5.3 Mukhiyas: Study of 30 Panchayats: Socio-economic and political profile of EWRs shows that 86.7 percent were in farming, 63 percent were in the age group of 35 to 60 years, 83 percent were Hindus, 46.7 percent belonged to OBCs, 23.3 percent belonged to the general category and 20 percent were SCs.

60 percent of the mukhiyas were literate and 26.7 percent mukhiyas had a high education but below the graduation level whereas 42.3 percent zilla parishad chairpersons had high school level education and 38.5 percent were graduates and above.

11.5.4 Involvement: The primary form of participation of EWRs was the involvement in the functioning of the meetings of the GPs. It was here that various problems of the GPs were discussed and through consensus or voting, the priorities were fixed for the GP's intervention. It is the only forum that can ensure a direct and participative democracy. It offers equal opportunity to all citizens of a village or cluster of villages to discuss and criticize, approve or reject proposals of the panchayat executive and also assess its performance. The decisions are taken by consensus.

The gram sabha meetings were being held regularly thrice a year as claimed by 90 percent of the mukhiyas. However, the following inadequacies were found.

1. The agenda for the meeting or minutes of the meeting (MoM) of the GP were not found.
2. The mukhayias claimed that the MoM were with the panchyat secretary who stays outside the village.
3. Many of the formally made decisions of the meetings were ignored for implementation.
4. Statutory standing committees were generally not formed and, even when formed, their meetings were not held.
5. Panchayat *sachiv* is generally not available either in his office or even the GP area.
6. Panchayat *sachiv* is often reluctant to provide information to the villagers on rules/programmes/circulars.

All the major decisions in gram sabha meetings were taken by mukhyia and if she is a female, she was influenced in the process by her husband, panchayat *sachives* or some non-governmental organisations. The presence of women in gram sabha meetings was found to be very thin. Gender concerns and preferences were never fully reflected in the proceedings of the gram sabha.

Many studies suggest that training is an important factor affecting the performance of elected women representatives. The primary data from Bihar show that 65 percent of elected women did not receive any training in their political term. 40 percent claimed that training was not held and 25 percent claimed that they were never called for it. High levels of satisfaction with different aspects of training (seating, visibility of screen board, training material, quality of instructors) among those who attended the training was found which further reinforces the importance of having a defined training programme for elected representatives.

It was also observed that EWRs prior political involvement and the experience of working with a SHG definitely had a critical impact on better performance. The EWRs also emphasized the importance of women specific training and that it should be organized regularly, covering multiple dimensions including rules and regulations, administrative issues, budgeting and finance and the implementation of development schemes.

The higher level of educational attainment does not seem to have played an important role in determining the performance in Bihar. Literacy was essential but higher education certainly did not help. 30.8 percent of the chairpersons at the zila parishad had a higher level of education and 75.4 percent of the mukhiyas had middle level education, but this gap did not show a significant positive correlation with better performance of elected women representatives. On the other hand, those who were illiterate or had been educated below the level of primary school also did not perform well.

The data shows that the duration (in years) of political involvement is directly proportionate to the performance of women representatives. We differentiate on the performance of women who hailed from families with political background and those who can be termed "first generation political aspirants" or women who drifted into PRIs due to the reservations. Even though the amendment made the "space" for both these groups to enter the PRIs, the speed with which they took to the new role, varied.

As women progress in their political career, they become better performers by virtue of being politically more aware and experienced. Thus, effort should be made not only to maintain the representation of women in politics in terms of their percentage, but also their ability to remain in politics. Membership of groups/committees plays an important role in terms of increasing the visibility of women in the village. A significant proportion of women representatives said that they were earlier associated with groups/committees and confirmed that this association helped them in joining politics. Thus, such entities should be provided greater support.

It was found that the non-governmental organizations and SHGs certainly played a crucial role in bringing about EWRs together, mobilizing them, building their capacity and preparing the ground for the network of elected women representatives for participation The females who had an earlier experience of working with the civil society were bringing their experience into governance at the local level and making the state and society sensitive to gender injustice, inequality and issue of poverty. The NGOs and civil society organizations were working with women representatives and building their network while also helping women representatives in their decision-making process in their day-to-day political aspects.

In Bihar, we have very strong traditional institutions and the new system coexists with them. The elders wield power in a way the Constitution may not have foreseen. If the PRIs are to succeed in their main goals, then they must work in harmony with these traditional institutions and not confront them head-on. This is easier said than done. The traditional institutions have not given space for women. Many of the factors that hindered women in the earlier system continue to exist and operate in rural areas. In fact, it was felt in course of our group discussions that gender as a phenomenon hardly ever appears in a pure form. It is almost always alloyed with caste, class and religious factors. In matters where there was a clash between gender and caste or class, it was impossible to expect women to align themselves with other women, going against their caste or class loyalties.

11.6 Recommendations

The study recommends the following for improving the quality of participation of women in the panchayats:

1. Since women are one of the neglected categories, there should be a separate sub-quorum for attendance of women at gram sabha meetings.
2. There must be special training for women at the gram

sabha level.

3. In addition to that, each village should have a mahila mandal and mahila sabhas should be encouraged to facilitate women's concerns which should be raised on a priority basis in meetings of gram sabhas and ward sabhas.
4. Political parties and social activists should be encouraged to create greater awareness among the women about the importance of PRS and the need for active participation in gram sabha meetings.
5. There should be a provision of women component plans in PRI budgets.
6. There should be a linkgage between self-help groups and PRIs at all levels.
7. Women candidates should be given an opportunity to serve full term.
8. All SC/ST/OBC persons should be encouraged to form self-help groups (SHGs). These bodies should be used to deliberate upon development needs of the village and the implementation of the development schemes approved. They should then decide the modalities of expressing the views of the weaker sections of the society in the gram sabha meetings.

Training programmes should ensure continuity and touch upon several aspects and not only on the basis of panchayati raj and knowledge about government schemes. The government training programmes lack a comprehensive and gender sensitive approach. The NGOs' training programmes are limited in terms of outreach and frequency, though strong on ideological front. Women face multiple oppressions and have to cope with additional problems of domestic responsibilities, travel expenses and patriarchal control on their mobility. The training package has to be more meaningful which imparts practical skills and encourages them to take on the political challenge.

Lack of empathy and support to PRIs by political and bureaucratic structures has created innumerable hurdles in the functioning of these agencies. Institutionalised inequalities and pressures sabotage attempts at capacity building of elected women representatives. It is important to create platforms that would act as pressure points to force powers that-be to bring about changes in attitudes and behaviour of political and bureaucratic executives towards women functionaries of PRIs .

Stressing the need for making these provisions truly effective, there is a critical necessity of empowering women and doing away with surrogate representatives for this purpose. "Training of women representatives must not begin with the promise that women are themselves responsible for the lack of social and cultural capital. The situation is a systematic failure. Therefore, even the trainer must start from what the participants know and then take them to the arena of the unknown...building up community support networks for women members should be an important component of training intervention" (RGF Task Force Report, 2001).

Emphasis on procedures and programmes, rather than political process and critical issues that women encounter, is not going to usher in a qualitative change in the participation of women. Majority of women representatives are now showing their determination to occupy public space and are fighting for their rights and legitimate space. In their struggle against entrenched systems disempowering them, they have to overcome many hurdles, such as conditions of poverty, social responsibility for the domestic unit, growing criminalisation of political process and interlocking of other social relations with gender relations. This is just a small beginning, though, and much remains to be done before we can actually claim to have empowered the women elected members of panchayati raj.

12

Local Governance Experiences of India and Pakistan*

12.1 Introduction

During October 2005, the Union Minister of Panchayati Raj, Shri Mani Shankar Aiyar, visited Pakistan and a dialogue commenced in the office of the Prime Minister of Pakistan, with the Chairman, National Reconstruction Bureau, in respect of the experience gained in India and Pakistan on local governance. In May 2006, Secretary, Ministry of Panchayati Raj, visited Pakistan and carried forward the deliberation with the Chairman, National Reconstruction Bureau, and his team of officials. During these discussions, a Pakistan-India Joint Working Group (JWG) on Local Governance was proposed at the official level, together with a Joint India-Pakistan Forum (JIPF) on Local Governance at the ministerial level, with Minister of Panchayati Raj and the Chairman, National Reconstruction Bureau as the co-chairman. The JWG would process and recommend a schedule of activities for bilateral exchanges between India and Pakistan to the JIPF. Typically, these activities would promote bilateral visits of local government elected representatives, and possibly other groups such as those wanting to promote rural tourism or rural business hubs in collaboration with elected structures of local government.

The general consensus that emerged through presentation and group discussion was that notwithstanding the progress made in India and Pakistan on decentralisation initiatives, a lot needs to be done. Implementation of the legislative changes initiated has by far been the biggest challenge facing us and mere amendments in legislative statutes would not stand the test of time unless we succeed in bringing a sea change in the mindset towards decentralisation. These pressing issues need to be addressed with alacrity and sincerity if we are to make sound progress on decentralisation initiatives.

12.2 Political Commitment and Sincerity

There is no gainsaying the fact that implementation of democratic decentralisation depends on the commitment of the political leadership, bureaucracy and the people. It is important to ensure that all stakeholders participate actively in decision-making including the poor and the marginalized. Civic engagement and transparency are not a panacea for all our ills but they can go a long way in addressing issues that incessantly plague us in our quest for a society based on the principles of equity, democracy, human rights and justice.

Decentralisation as a process should be central to all our planning paradigms and should be an integral part of our governance. It should not be a mere aspect of our policy but should be the core of our thinking. We need to have a holistic approach towards adopting it and concerted efforts are needed to ensure that it becomes the locus of our governance activities.

There is a silent revolution going on and people want to raise their voice and find their place in the development process. Most importantly, it has included the marginalized sections, in the process of governance. A large number of women and other marginalized classes came to power as a consequence of reservation provided to them in panchayats. Slowly but steadily, these groups have found a place in Indian polity and a new broad-based political leadership and wisdom is emerging. There have been achievements in building confidence and it has rekindled the hopes of the local citizenry.

12.3 Features of Local Governments in Pakistan

There are particular features of the Pakistan system of local government, which would bear reflecting upon in India. Like our panchayat, they have a union council at the village level, tehsil council (similar to mandal parishad in the State) at the next level and finally the district council similar to the zilla parishad in the State. Pakistan has four provinces and each Provincial Government has considerable influence on the village administration, but it is the union council, which has the final say in the implementation.

Union council is elected in a democratic manner and has 33 to 50 percent reservation for women and five percent reservations for minorities. "This should clear the misconception that women do not have a say in that country". There is political awareness among people there, but when it comes to implementation of reforms or devolution of powers, the subject is debatable.

The fundamental difference between the two systems as it came out from the discussion is that whereas panchayati raj in India is designed to strengthen the totality of our democratic institutions and practices, the Pakistan system of local governance is designed to strengthen elected institutions at the grassroots, to the detriment and disadvantage of democracy at the Provincial and National level. Second, in sharp contradiction to the long, somewhat tortured, and detailed provisions for panchayati raj worked into our Constitution through a process of consensus-building, local governance in Pakistan is governed by an ordinance issued a few years ago. This makes the future of local governments in Pakistan tied to the fortunes of the present regime. On the other hand, technically speaking, the design for devolution in the four provinces of Pakistan is so well structured that it has yielded considerable results in a much shorter period than in India and, therefore, is likely to be continued into successor regimes albeit with modifications.

The system of governance inherited by both the countries had its roots in the feudal-imperial legacy of the past, largely modified and adapted by the British to meet their colonial ends. The efforts of leaders of freedom struggle who upheld the principle of self-reliant villages did not reflect much in the new constitutions framed after Independence. Pakistan is generally seen as an over centralized politico-administrative federal structure with the local bodies merely as appendages.

Over the years, local governments were never established as organs of the state. The provincial governments created instrument for exercising management and financial control over the local bodies through their own local government departments. This system continued till the chief executive of Pakistan defined devolution as one of the seven main objectives of the government on October 17, 1999 and formed National Reconstruction Bureau with the mission of reconstituting the institutions for establishing democracy at three levels—federal, provincial and local. It has chosen to start at the bottom—the local level and take the bottom up approach to establish genuine democracy at all levels. Three months of concerted efforts finally led to the promulgation of a plan for devolution of power at the grassroots level. By August 14, 2001, elections were held and local governments were in position in all districts of the provinces in Pakistan. A transition is on. It is not an easy task to upturn an order that has been deep-rooted over a period of decades in a short span of 5 years.

Pakistan has suffered cyclical problems of governance stemming from a weak political culture and an overdeveloped state (basically colonial in its origins and present functioning) together with several economic distortions, numerous ideological dissensions and regional challenges. The main challenges for the new regime are to establish a tenable legitimacy to construct a broadly acceptable system of accountability and to induct a transparent system of governance based on proper constitutional and electoral norms. Pakistan's overall political and economic situation is becoming more complex, dispiriting and confusing.

12.4 Local Governance in India

In India, the local governance system had no Constitutional backing till the Seventy-third and Seventy-fourth Constitutional amendments of 1993. With the passing of

Conformity Act, all the states and union territories are expected to initiate activities for decentralization. The devolution of powers to the panchayati raj institutions in different states has not been uniform. A few states like Kerala, Karnataka and West Bengal did much to devolve 3Fs (funds, functions and functionaries) at the grassroots level. But in most of the states, a great deal of confusion as regards the nature of the transfer itself prevailed. It was at a time when there was no proper guidance to go ahead, the UPA government for the first time created a central ministry to oversee, facilitate and ensure that the Seventy-third Constitutional amendment is observed in letter and spirit.

The first step in defining the scope of the ministry was taken at the conference of chief ministers of the States in which the Prime Minister of India stressed that effective and sustainable poverty alleviation could be achieved only by empowering PRIs. In pursuance of the decision taken at the conference of chief ministers in June 2004, the MoPR organized a series of seven round tables of state ministers of panchayati raj for detailed deliberations on the blueprint for future action. Within a period of 150 days, consensus was achieved among all state and union territories on a compendium of resolutions covering 18 jointly identified dimensions of the panchayati raj and comprising 150 key steps which remained to be done. The Ministry also initiated several steps for interacting with other similar bodies internationally both to learn from the best practices. The initiative of the Ministry covers three areas, namely, bilateral cooperation with other countries, interaction with multilateral agencies and linking up with common forum dealing with local self-government.

After 14 years of the Constitutional mandate, our steel frame of colonial administration is still intact; there are no benchmarks for pushing effective fiscal decentralization; and, the provincial continues to obstruct the growth of the local in India.

The strength of democratic durability is based on its rootedness; both institutions and culture of democracy are important. If concrete and urgent steps towards making local governance in India are not taken by the political and official class now, it may be difficult to contain the spread of popular disaffection and violence any further.

12.5 Global Experiences of Local Governments

How to place people at the centre of development and governance processes is a global concern. The near universal lack of faith in the political system, governments, political parties, and politicians is due to many factors. Centralization, money politics, and corruption make a government top-down and unresponsive.

At their worst, governments are more of a threat than a benefit, especially for the poor. At their best, governments are still not considered responsive to the interests of the citizenry beyond those of powerful interest groups. The crisis of confidence in government leads to alienation and low levels of citizen participation, creating a vicious circle of even more top-down and less responsive government. The virtuous circle that can replace it consists of an enabling environment for significant citizen empowerment, participation, and representation, making government increasingly bottom-up and responsive.

In most of the countries of the world, local governments are an extended version of the state or provincial government with much dependency syndrome. Their role mainly confines to the delivery of civic services and providing basic amenities only. The countries opting for local governments are in search of good role models. In the South Asian region, there is a proactive stand favouring decentralization. It is the need of the hour to provide them with relevant information on their way forward.

There is evidence across nations that globalisation, while leading to higher levels of GDP growth, has neither been socially benign nor instrumental in reducing poverty of the masses both in the developed and developing economies. In India and Pakistan too, it has now been accepted that higher GDP rates during the recent years have not helped the larger masses in getting integrated with the process of development. It is important that local governance be brought centre stage as the principal governance reform to reinforce economic reforms in such a manner as to secure inclusive growth. Inclusive growth "is growth pro-poor". The bulk of the population of this country feels that they have not benefited in any obvious way from the development of the last decade. There is need to reconceptualise inclusion as not only recognizing the usual marginalized communities or sections of the society as beneficiaries but by including them as thinkers who think and "know" differently, and whose presence in designing, is the real inclusion. There is need to give the excluded agency inclusion—to include knowledge and analysis and experience of minority groups, women and other excluded and deprived sections of society, in development design.

To sum up, the Indo-Pakistan relation can be consolidated under this framework, which recognizes and facilitates the principles of democracy, diversity, pluralism, and federalism, and uses them as pillars of consolidation rather than succumb to the temptations of fragmentation. Both the states must empower their local self-governance to bridge the political, social, religious, and economic differences that may have cropped up or been accentuated by and after partition—the differences must be allowed to persist, flourish, or decline organically unless they challenge the fundamental rubric of the state. Reunification would entail changes that would call for tremendous devolution of power, and unfortunately significant changes generally have greater chance of success when there is opportunity to seize power than to give it away.

For reunification to be successful, the central governments in both the countries must be prepared to lose much of their control over states and provinces, the states and provinces in turn must be willing to confer much greater authority to local bodies, and local bodies must allow power to dissolve within the general populace.

*This chapter is based on the presentations made at Pakistan-India Symposium on Local Governance, held in Lahore from July 1-3, 2007.

Appendix

National Policy for Empowerment of Women (NPEW)

Progress towards gender equality and women's empowerment in India has been built upon strong commitments by the government and unflagging effort by the women's movement. India's commitment to gender equality is further evidenced by the fact that it is a signatory to Convention on the Elimination of All Forms of Discrimination against Women (CEDAW), which was ratified on June 25, 1993 (with one reservation and two declaratory statements). India is also a signatory to the Convention on the Rights of the Child. The first report to the UN Committee of Experts on the Rights of the Child was submitted in 2000 and the second report in 2004.

In pursuance of the avowed objective of empowering the *women* as agents of socio-economic change, the National Policy on Empowerment of Women was adopted in April 2001. Gender inequality arising out of social norms and cultural traditions has been addressed through a range of direct and indirect measures, and the aim of the NPEW has been to bring about social change—changes in attitudes towards women, and women's empowerment. The policy itself reflects the aspirations of women and the women's movement. The effort is to bring gender justice and make *de jure* equality into *de facto* equality. Several State Governments have also formulated a policy for women's empowerment.

On the basis of NPEW, the National Plan of Action is being implemented which includes the following strategies:

1. To create an enabling environment for women to exercise their rights both within and outside their homes.
2. To reserve one-third of seats for women in the Lok Sabha and State Legislative Assemblies.

3. To adopt a special strategy for Women Component Plan to ensure that at least 30 percent of funds and benefits flow to women from all development sectors.
4. To organize women in self-help groups as a mark of the beginning of empowering them.
5. To accord high priority and ensure easy access to maternal and child health services.
6. To initiate steps for eliminating gender bias in all educational programmes; further to institute plans for free education of girls up to college levels including professional levels.
7. To equip women with necessary skills in modern upcoming trades which would make them economically independent and self-reliant.
8. To increase women's access to credit through setting up of a development bank for women entrepreneurs in small and tiny sectors.

Various aspects of NPEW are as under.

A.1 Introduction

The principle of gender equality is enshrined in the Indian Constitution in its Preamble, Fundamental Rights, Fundamental Duties and Directive Principles of State Policy. The Constitution not only grants equality to women, but also empowers the State to adopt measures of positive discrimination in favour of women. Since Independence in 1947, there has been a marked shift in the approach to issues related to welfare, development and empowerment of women. Within the framework of a democratic polity, India's laws, development policies, schemes/programmes under Five Year Plans have aimed at advancement of women in different spheres. In recent years, the empowerment of women has been recognized as the central issue in determining the status of women. The National Commission for Women was set up by an Act of Parliament in 1990 to safeguard the rights and legal entitlements of women. The Seventy-third and Seventy-fourth Amendments to the Constitution of India provided for reservation of seats for women in panchayats and municipalities, laying a strong foundation for their participation in decision-making at the local levels.

India has also ratified various international conventions and human rights instruments committing to secure equal rights for women. Key among them is the ratification of the Convention on Elimination of All Forms of Discrimination against Women (CEDAW) in 1993.

The Mexico Plan of Action (1975), the Nairobi Forward Looking Strategies (1985), the Beijing Declaration as well as the Platform for Action (1995) and the Outcome Document— adopted by the General Assembly Session of the United Nations on Gender Equality and Development and Peace for the 21st Century— titled "Further Actions and Initiatives to Implement the Beijing Declaration and the Platform for Action" have been unreservedly endorsed by India for appropriate follow up.

A.2 Objectives of the Policy

National Policy for Empowerment of Women, 2001 was formulated for bringing about advancement, development and empowerment of women in all spheres of life through creation of a more responsive judicial and legal system sensitive to women and mainstreaming a gender perspective in the development process. The strengthening and formation of relevant institutional mechanisms and implementation of international obligations/commitments and co-operation at the international, regional and sub-regional level was another commitment.

The primary objective of NPEW was to bring about the advancement, development and empowerment of women. Specifically, the objectives of this Policy included the following:

1. Creating an environment through positive economic and social policies for full development of women to enable

them to realize their full potential.

2. The *de jure* and *de facto* enjoyment of all human rights and fundamental freedom by women on equal basis with men in all spheres—political, economic, social, cultural and civil.
3. Equal access to participation and decision-making of women in social, political and economic life of the nation.
4. Equal access to women to healthcare, quality education at all levels, career and vocational guidance, employment, equal remuneration, occupational health and safety, social security and public office etc.
5. Strengthening legal systems aimed at elimination of all forms of discrimination against women.
6. Changing societal attitudes and community practices by active participation and involvement of both men and women.
7. Mainstreaming a gender perspective in the development process.
8. Elimination of discrimination and all forms of violence against women and the girl child.
9. Building and strengthening partnerships with civil society, particularly women's organizations.

A.3 Various Elements of NPEW

A.3.1 Politico-legal Empowerment of Women

A.3.1.1 Legal-Judicial System: Legal-judicial system would be made more responsive and gender sensitive to women's needs, especially in cases of domestic violence and personal assault. New laws would be enacted and existing laws reviewed to ensure that justice is quick and the punishment meted out to the culprits is commensurate with the severity of the offence.

At the initiative of and with the full participation of all stakeholders including community and religious leaders, NPEW would aim to encourage changes in personal laws such as those related to marriage, divorce, maintenance and guardianship so as to eliminate discrimination against women.

The evolution of property rights in a patriarchal system has contributed to the subordinate status of women. NPEW would aim to encourage changes in laws relating to ownership of property and inheritance by evolving consensus in order to make them gender just.

A.3.1.2 Decision-making: Women's equality in power sharing and active participation in decision-making, including decision-making in political process at all levels would be ensured for the achievement of the goals of empowerment. All measures would be taken to guarantee women, equal access to and full participation in decision-making bodies at every level, including the legislative, executive, judicial, corporate, statutory bodies, as also the advisory commissions, committees, boards, trusts etc. Affirmative action such as reservations/quotas, including in higher legislative bodies, will be considered whenever necessary on a time-bound basis. Women-friendly personnel policies will also be drawn up to encourage women to participate effectively in the developmental process.

A3.1.3 Mainstreaming a Gender Perspective in the Development Process: Policies, programmes and systems would be established to ensure mainstreaming of women's perspectives in all developmental processes, as catalysts, participants and recipients. Wherever there are gaps in policies and programmes, women-specific interventions would be undertaken to bridge these. Coordinating and monitoring mechanisms will also be devised to assess, from time to time, the progress of such mainstreaming mechanisms. Issues and concerns related to women would be specifically addressed and reflected in all concerned laws, sectoral policies, plans and programmes of action.

A.3.2 Economic Empowerment of Women:

A.3.2.1 Poverty Eradication: Since women comprise the majority of the population below the poverty line and are very often in situations of extreme poverty—given the harsh realities of intra-household and social discrimination—macro economic policies and poverty eradication programmes would specifically address the needs and problems of such women. There would be improved implementation of programmes which are already women-oriented with special targets for women. Steps would be taken for mobilization of poor women and convergence of services, by offering them a range of economic and social options, along with necessary support measures to enhance their capabilities

A.3.2.2 Micro Credit: In order to enhance women's access to credit for consumption and production, establishment of new and strengthening of existing micro-credit mechanisms and micro-finance institutions would be undertaken so that the outreach of credit is enhanced. Other supportive measures would be taken to ensure adequate flow of credit through extant financial institutions and banks so that all women below poverty line have easy access to credit.

A.3.2.3 Women and Economy: Women's perspectives would be included in designing and implementing macroeconomic and social policies by institutionalizing their participation in such processes. Their contribution to socio-economic development as producers and workers would be recognized in the formal and informal sectors (including home-based workers) and appropriate policies relating to employment and to her working conditions would be drawn up. Such measures could include the following:

1. Reinterpretation and redefinition of conventional concepts of work wherever necessary (e.g. in the census records), to reflect contribution of women as producers and workers.
2. Preparation of satellite and national accounts.
3. Development of appropriate methodologies for undertaking (1) and (2) above.

A.3.2.4 Globalization: Globalization—the gender impact of which has not been evaluated fully—has presented new challenges for the realization of the goal of women's equality. It is evident that there is a need for re-framing policies for access to employment and quality of employment.

Benefits of the growing global economy have been unevenly distributed leading to wider economic disparities, the feminization of poverty, increased gender inequality through deteriorating working conditions and unsafe working environment especially in the informal economy and rural areas. Strategies would be designed to enhance the capacity of women and empower them to meet the negative social and economic impacts, which may flow from the globalization process.

A.3.2.5 Women and Agriculture: In view of the critical role of women in the agriculture and allied sectors as producers, concentrated efforts would be made to ensure that benefits of various programmes/schemes reach them in proportion to their numbers. The programmes for training women in soil conservation, social forestry, dairy development and other occupations allied to agriculture (like horticulture, livestock including small animal husbandry, poultry, fisheries etc.) would be expanded to benefit women workers in the agriculture sector.

A.3.2.6 Women and Industry: The important role played by women in electronics, information technology, food processing, agro industry and textiles has been crucial for the development of these sectors. They would be given comprehensive support in terms of labour legislation, social security and other support services to participate in various industrial sectors.

Women at present cannot work in night shift in factories even if they wish to. Suitable measures will be taken to enable women to work on the night shift in factories. This would be accompanied with support services for security, transportation etc.

A.3.2.7 Support Services: The provision of support services for women—like child care facilities, including crèches at work places and educational institutions, homes for the aged and the disabled—would be expanded and improved to create an enabling environment and to ensure their full cooperation in social, political and economic life. Women-friendly personnel policies would also be drawn up to encourage women to participate effectively in the developmental process.

A.3.3 Social Empowerment of Women:

A.3.3.1 Education: Equal access to education for women and girls would be ensured. Special measures would be taken to eliminate discrimination, universalize education, eradicate illiteracy, create a gender-sensitive educational system, increase enrolment and retention rates of girls and improve the quality of education to facilitate life-long learning as well as development of occupation/vocation/technical skills by women. Reducing the gender gap in secondary and higher education would be a focus area. Sectoral time targets in existing policies would be achieved, with a special focus on girls and women, particularly those belonging to weaker sections including the scheduled castes/scheduled tribes/other backward classes/minorities. Gender sensitive curricula would be developed at all levels of educational system in order to address sex stereotyping as one of the causes of gender discrimination.

A.3.3.2 Health: A holistic approach to women's health which includes both nutrition and health services would be adopted and special attention would be given to the needs of women and the girls at all stages of the life cycle. The reduction of infant mortality and maternal mortality, which are sensitive indicators of human development, is a priority concern. NPEW reiterated the national demographic goals for infant mortality rate (IMR), maternal mortality rate (MMR) set out in the National Population Policy, 2000. Women should have access to comprehensive, affordable and quality health care. Measures would be adopted that take into account the reproductive rights of women to enable them to exercise informed choices, their vulnerability to sexual and health problems together with endemic, infectious and communicable diseases such as malaria, TB, and water-borne diseases as well as hypertension and cardio-pulmonary diseases. The social, developmental and health consequences of HIV/AIDS and other sexually transmitted diseases would be tackled from a gender perspective.

To effectively meet problems of infant and maternal mortality, and early marriage, the availability of good and accurate data at micro level on deaths, birth and marriages is required. Strict implementation of registration of births and deaths would be ensured and registration of marriages would be made compulsory.

In accordance with the commitment of the National Population Policy, 2000 to population stabilization, NPEW recognized the critical need of men and women to have access to safe, effective and affordable methods of family planning of their choice and the need to suitably address the issues of early marriages and spacing of children. Interventions such as spread of education, compulsory registration of marriage should impact on delaying the age of marriage so that by 2010 child marriages are eliminated.

Women's traditional knowledge about health care and nutrition would be recognized through proper documentation and its use would be encouraged. The use of Indian and alternative systems of medicine would be enhanced within the framework of overall health infrastructure available for women.

A.3.3.3 Nutrition: In view of the high risk of malnutrition and disease that women face at all the three critical stages, viz. infancy and childhood, adolescent and reproductive phase, focussed attention would be paid to meeting the nutritional needs of women at all stages of the life cycle. This is also important in view of the critical link between the health of adolescent girls, pregnant and lactating women with the health of infant and young children. Special efforts would be made to tackle the problem of macro and micro nutrient deficiencies especially amongst pregnant and lactating women as it leads to various diseases and disabilities.

Intra-household discrimination in nutritional matters vis-à-vis girls and women would be sought to be ended through appropriate strategies. Widespread use of nutrition education would be made to address the issues of intra-household imbalances in nutrition and the special needs of pregnant and lactating women. Women's participation would also be ensured in the planning, superintendence and delivery of the system.

A.3.3.4 Drinking Water and Sanitation: Special attention would be given to the needs of women in the provision of safe drinking water, sewage disposal, toilet facilities and sanitation within accessible reach of households, especially in rural areas and urban slums. Women's participation would be ensured in the planning, delivery and maintenance of such services.

A.3.3.5 Housing and Shelter: Women's perspectives would be included in housing policies, planning of housing colonies and provision of shelter both in rural and urban areas. Special attention would be given for providing adequate and safe housing and accommodation for women including single women, heads of households, working women, students, apprentices and trainees.

A.3.3.6 Environment: Women would be involved and their perspectives reflected in the policies and programmes for environment, conservation and restoration. Considering the impact of environmental factors on their livelihoods, women's participation would be ensured in the conservation of the environment and control of environmental degradation. The vast majority of rural women still depend on the locally available non-commercial sources of energy such as animal dung, crop waste and fuel wood. In order to ensure the efficient use of these energy resources in an environmental friendly manner, NPEW would aim at promoting the programmes of non-conventional energy resources. Women would be involved in spreading the use of solar energy, biogas, smokeless *chulahs* and other rural application so as to have a visible impact of these measures in influencing ecosystem and in changing the life styles of rural women.

A.3.3.7 Science and Technology: Programmes would be strengthened to bring about a greater involvement of women in science and technology. These would include measures to motivate girls to take up science and technology for higher education and also ensure that development projects with scientific and technical inputs involve women fully. Efforts to develop a scientific temper and awareness would also be stepped up. Special measures would be taken for their training in areas where they have special skills like communication and information technology. Efforts to develop appropriate technologies suited to women's needs as well as to reduce their drudgery would be given a special focus too.

A.3.3.8 Women in Difficult Circumstances: In recognition of the diversity of women's situations and in acknowledgement of the needs of disadvantaged groups, measures and programmes would be undertaken to provide them with special assistance. These groups include women in extreme poverty, destitute women, women in conflict situations, women affected by natural calamities, women in less developed regions, the disabled widows, elderly women, single women in difficult circumstances, women heading households, those displaced from employment, migrants, women who are victims of marital violence, deserted women and prostitutes etc.

A.3.3.9 Violence against Women: All forms of violence against women, physical and mental, whether at domestic or societal levels, including those arising from customs, traditions or accepted practices shall be dealt with effectively with a view to eliminate its incidence. Institutions and mechanisms for assistance would be created and strengthened for prevention of such violence—including sexual harassment at work place—and for the rehabilitation of the victims of violence and for taking effective action against the perpetrators of such violence. A special emphasis would also be laid on programmes and measures to deal with trafficking in women and girls.

A.3.3.10 Rights of the Girl Child: All forms of discrimination against the girl child and violation of her rights shall be eliminated by undertaking strong measures both preventive and punitive within and outside the family. These would relate specifically to strict enforcement of laws against prenatal sex selection and the practices of female foeticide, female infanticide, child marriage, child abuse and child prostitution etc. Removal of discrimination in the treatment of the girl child within the family and outside and projection of a positive image of the girl child would be actively fostered. There would be special emphasis on the needs of the girl child and earmarking of substantial investments in the areas relating to food and nutrition, health and education, and in vocational education. In implementing programmes for eliminating child labour, there would be a special focus on girl children.

A.3.3.11 Mass Media: Media would be used to portray images consistent with human dignity of girls and women. NPEW would specifically strive to remove demeaning, degrading and negative conventional stereotypical images of women and violence against women. Private sector partners and media networks would be involved at all levels to ensure equal access for women, particularly in the area of information and communication technologies. The media would be encouraged to develop codes of conduct, professional guidelines and other self-regulatory mechanisms to remove gender stereotypes and promote balanced portrayals of women and men.

A.4 Operational Strategies of NPEW

A.4.1 Action Plans: All Central and State Ministries would draw up time bound action plans for translating NPEW into a set of concrete actions, through a participatory process in consultation with Central/State Departments of Women and

Child Development and National/State Commissions for Women. The Plans would specifically include the following:

1. Measurable goals to be achieved by 2010.
2. Identification and commitment of resources.
3. Responsibilities for implementation of action points.
4. Structures and mechanisms to ensure efficient monitoring, review and gender impact assessment of action points and policies.
5. Introduction of a gender perspective in the budgeting process.

In order to support better planning and programme formulation and adequate allocation of resources, gender development indices (GDI) would be developed by networking with specialized agencies. These could be analyzed and studied in depth. Gender auditing and development of evaluation mechanisms would also be undertaken along side.

Collection of gender disaggregated data by all primary data collecting agencies of the Central and State Governments as well as research and academic institutions in the public and private sectors would be undertaken. Data and information gaps in vital areas reflecting the status of women would be sought to be filled in by these immediately. All Ministries/corporations/banks and financial institutions etc. would be advised to collect, collate, disseminate and maintain/publish data related to programmes and benefits on a gender disaggregated basis. This would help in meaningful planning and evaluation of policies.

A.4.2 Institutional Mechanisms: Institutional mechanisms, to promote the advancement of women, which exist at the Central and State levels, would be strengthened. This would be done through appropriate and would relate to, among others, provision of adequate resources, training and skills to effectively influence macro policies, legislations, programmes etc. to achieve the empowerment of women.

National and State Councils would be formed to oversee the operationalisation of the Policy on a regular basis. The

National Council would be headed by the Prime Minister and the State Councils by the chief ministers and would be broad in composition having representatives from the concerned departments/ministries, national and state commissions for women, social welfare boards, representatives of non-governmental organizations, women's organisations, corporate sector, trade unions, financing institutions, academics, experts and social activists. These bodies would review the progress made in implementing the Policy twice a year. The National Development Council would also be informed, from time to time, of the progress of the programme undertaken under the policy for advice and comments.

National and state resource centres on women would be established with mandates for collection and dissemination of information, undertaking research work, conducting surveys, implementing training and awareness generation programmes etc. These centres would link up with women's studies centres and other research and academic institutions through suitable information networking systems.

While institutions at the district level would be strengthened, women would be helped by Government at the grassroots level through its programmes to organize and strengthen self-help groups (SHGs) at the anganwadi, village and town levels. The women's groups would be helped to institutionalize themselves into registered societies and to federate at the panchayat/municipal level. These societies would bring about synergistic implementation of all the social and economic development programmes by drawing resources made available through Government and non-government channels, including banks and financial institutions and by establishing a close interface with the panchayats/ municipalities.

A.4.3 Resource Management: Availability of adequate financial, human and market resources to implement NPEW would be managed by concerned departments, financial credit institutions and banks, private sector, civil society and other connected institutions. This process would include the following:

1. Assessment of benefits flowing to women and resource allocation to the programmes relating to them through an exercise of gender budgeting. Appropriate changes in policies would be made to optimize benefits to women under these schemes.
2. Adequate resource allocation to develop and promote the policy outlined earlier based on (1) above by concerned departments.
3. Developing synergy between personnel of health, rural development, education and women and child development department at field level and other village level functionaries.
4. Meeting credit needs by banks and financial credit institutions through suitable policy initiatives and development of new institutions in coordination with the Department of Women and Child Development.

The strategy of Women's Component Plan adopted in the Ninth Five Year Plan (1997-98 to 2001-02) ensured that not less than 30 percent of benefits/funds flow to women from all ministries and departments would be implemented effectively so that the needs and interests of women and girls are addressed by all concerned sectors. The Department of Women and Child Development being the nodal ministry will monitor and review the progress of the implementation of the Component Plan from time to time in terms of both quality and quantity in collaboration with the Planning Commission.

Efforts would be made to channelize private sector investments also, to support programmes and projects for advancement of women.

A.4.4 Legislation: The existing legislative structure would be reviewed and additional legislative measures taken by identified departments to implement the Policy. This would also involve a review of all existing laws including personal, customary and tribal laws, subordinate legislation, related rules as well as executive and administrative regulations to eliminate all gender discriminatory references. The process would be planned over a time period from 2000 to 2003. The specific measures required would be evolved through a consultation process involving civil society, National Commission for Women, and Department of Women and Child Development. In appropriate cases, the consultation process would be widened to include other stakeholders also.

Effective implementation of legislations would be promoted by involving civil society and community. Appropriate changes in legislations would be undertaken, if necessary. In addition, following other specific measures would be taken to implement the legislation effectively:

1. Strict enforcement of all relevant legal provisions and speedy redressal of grievances would be ensured, with a special focus on violence and gender related atrocities.
2. Measures to prevent and punish sexual harassment at the place of work, protection for women workers in the organized/unorganized sector and strict enforcement of relevant laws such as Equal Remuneration Act and Minimum Wages Act would be undertaken.
3. Crimes against women, their incidence, prevention, investigation, detection and prosecution would be regularly reviewed at all crime review fora and conferences at the central, state and district levels. Recognised, local, voluntary organizations would be authorized to lodge complaints and facilitate registration, investigations and legal proceedings related to violence and atrocities against girls and women.
4. Women's cells in police stations, women police stations, family courts, mahila courts, counselling centres, legal aid centres and nyaya panchayats would be strengthened and expanded to eliminate violence and atrocities against women.
5. Widespread dissemination of information on all aspects of legal rights, human rights and other entitlements of

women, through specially designed legal literacy programmes and rights information programmes would be done.

A.4.5 Gender Sensitization: Training of personnel of executive, legislative and judicial wings of the State—with a special focus on policy and programme framers, implementation and development agencies, law enforcement machinery and the judiciary, as well as non-governmental organizations—would be undertaken. Other measures would include the following:

1. Promoting societal awareness of gender issues and women's human rights.
2. Review of curriculum and educational materials to include gender education and human rights issues.
3. Removal of all references derogatory to the dignity of women from all public documents and legal instruments.
4. Use of different forms of mass media to communicate social messages relating to women's equality and empowerment.

A.4.6 Panchayati Raj Institutions: The Seventy-third and Seventy-fourth Amendments to the Indian Constitution have served as a breakthrough towards ensuring equal access and increased participation of women in political power structure. The PRIs would play a central role in the process of enhancing women's participation in public life. The PRIs and the local self-governments would be actively involved in the implementation and execution of NPEW at the grassroots level.

A.4.7 Partnership with the Voluntary Sector Organizations: The involvement of voluntary organizations, associations, federations, trade unions, non-governmental organizations, women's organizations, as well as institutions dealing with education, training and research would be ensured in the formulation, implementation, monitoring and review of all policies and programmes affecting women. Towards this end, they would be provided with appropriate support related to resources and capacity building and facilitated to participate actively in the process of the empowerment of women.

A.4.8 International Cooperation: NPEW would aim at implementation of international obligations/commitments in all sectors on empowerment of women such as the Convention on All Forms of Discrimination against Women (CEDAW), Convention on the Rights of the Child (CRC), International Conference on Population and Development (ICPD) and other such instruments. International, regional and sub-regional cooperation towards the empowerment of women would continue to be encouraged through sharing of experiences, exchange of ideas and technology, networking with institutions and organizations and through bilateral and multilateral partnerships.

Bibliography/References

Bibliography

Agnihotri, V.K., S. Krishna and A. Mukherjee (1994), "Human Resource Development for Panchayats", in Amitava Mukherjee (ed.) Decentralisation and Panchayats in the Nineties, Vikas Publications, New Delhi.

Aiyar, Mani Shankar (2002), "Panchayati Raj: The Way Forward", *Economic and Political Weekly*, Vol. 37, No. 31, August, pp. 3293-3297.

Alsop, Ruth, et al. (2001), "Inclusion and Local Elected Governments: The Panchayati Raj System in India", Social Development Paper 37, World Bank, South Asia Region, Social Development Unit, Washington DC.

Andhra Pradesh Academy of Rural Development (2002), "Manual for Management of Gram Panchayats", Hyderabad.

Anveshi, H. (1993), "Reworking Gender relations, Redefining Politics, Nellore Village Women against Arrack", *Economic and Political Weekly*, January, pp. 16-23.

Athreya, V.B., B.S. Bhargava and Manu Bhaskar (1992), "Women in Grassroots Democracy: A Study of Kerala", University of Kerala/ ICSSR, New Delhi.

Bandyopadhyay, D., Saila K. Ghosh and Buddhadeb Ghosh (2003), "Dependency versus Autonomy: Identity Crisis of India's Panchayats", *Economic and Political Weekly*, Vol. 38, No. 38, pp. 3984-3991.

Bardhan, Pranab K., Dilip Mookherjee and Monica Parra Torrado (2010), "Impact of Political Reservations in West Bengal Local Governments on Anti-Poverty Targeting", *Journal of Globalization and Development*, Vol. 1, Issue 1.

Behar, Amitabh and Yamini Aiyar (2003), "Networks of Panchayat Women: Civil Society Space for Political Action", *Economic and Political Weekly*, Vol. 38, No. 47, pp. 4936-4940.

Besley, Timothy, Rohini Pande, Lupin Rahman and Vijayendra Rao (2004), "The Politics of Public Good Provision: Evidence from Indian Local Governments", *Journal of the European Economic Association*, Vol. 2, Nos. 2/3, pp. 416-426.

Blair, Harry (2000), "Participation and Accountability at the Periphery: Democratic Local Governance in Six Countries",

World Development, Vol. 28, No. 1, pp. 21-39.

Bohra, O.P. (2000), "Decentralisation and Devolution of Powers and Functions to Panchayats", *Journal of Rural Development*, Vol. 19(2).

Bryld, E. (2001), "Increasing Participation in Democratic Institutions through Decentralization: Empowering Women and Scheduled Castes and Tribes through Panchayat Raj in Rural India", *Democratization*, Vol. 8, No. 3, pp. 149-172.

Buch, Nirmala (2000), "Women's Experience in New Panchayats: The Emerging Leadership of Rural Women", Occasional Paper No. 35, Centre for Women's Development Studies, New Delhi.

Buch, Nirmala (2005), "Women and Panchayats: Opportunities, Challenges and Support", in L.C. Jain (ed.), Decentralization and Local Governance, New Delhi: Orient Longman.

Centre for Rural Studies and National Society for Promotion of Development Administration (2002), "Capacity Building of the PRIs in Uttaranchal State", Mussoorie, Uttaranchal: Centre for Rural Studies and National Society for Promotion of Development Administration.

Centre for Women's Development Studies (1999), "From Oppression to Assertion: A Study of Panchayats and Women in M.P., Rajasthan and U.P.", CWDS, New Delhi.

Chandrasekhar and Committee on Status of Women in India (CSWI) (1974), "Towards Equality", Ministry of Education and Social Welfare, Government of India.

Chattopadhyay, Raghabendra and Esther Duflo (2004), "Impact of Reservation in Panchayati Raj: Evidence from a Nationwide Randomised Experiment", *Economic and Political Weekly*, Vol. 39, No. 9, pp. 979-986.

Duflo, Esther (2005), "Why Political Reservations?", *Journal of the European Economic Association*, Vol. 3, Nos. 2/3, papers and proceedings of the Nineteenth Annual Congress of the European Economic Association, pp. 668-678.

Dutt, Kuntala Lahiri and Samanta Gopa (2002), "State Initiatives for the Empowerment of the Women of Rural Communities: Experiences from Eastern India", *Community Development Journal*, Vol. 37, No. 2, April, pp. 137-156.

Ebert, Fredrich (1993), "Shifting Women in Politics: Forms and Process", New Delhi, Har Anand Publication, New Delhi.

Everett, Jana (2009), "Governance Reforms and Rural Women in

India: What Type of Women Citizens Are Produced by the Will to Empower?", *Social Politics*, Vol. 16, Issue 2, pp. 279-302.

Fernandes, Aureliano (2003), "Aggrandiser Government and Local Governance", *Economic and Political Weekly*, Vol. 38, No. 27, July, pp. 2873-2879.

Flammang, Janet (ed.) (1984), "Political Women: Current Role in State and Local Government", Sage Publications, London.

Fredrick, Ebert, M.L. Goyal (1974), "Political Participation in a Developing Nation", India Asia Publishing House, Bombay.

Gleason, Suzanne (2001), "Female Political Participation and Health in India", Annals of the American Academy of Political and Social Science, *Culture and Development: International Perspectives*, Vol. 573, January, pp. 105-126.

Gupta, Shaibal (2001), "New Panchayats and Subaltern Resurgence", *Economic and Political Weekly*, Vol. 36, No. 29, July, pp. 2742-2744.

Gurumurthy, C. (1987), "Panchayati Raj and Weaker Sections", Ashish Publications, New Delhi.

Jain, L.C. (1994), "Panchayat: Women Will Win", *Kurukshetra*, June.

Jain, Devaki (1996), "Panchayat Raj: Women Changing Governance", Gender in Development Monograph Series #5, UNDP, New York.

Jain, Devaki (1992), "Women: New Vision of Leadership", presentation at Global Forum, Dublin, July.

Jayal, Niraja Gopal (2006), "Engendering Local Democracy: The Impact of Quotas for Women in India's Panchayats", *Democratization*, 13:1, pp. 15-35.

Jhamtani, A. (1995), "Rural Women: Powerless Partner in Development", *Kurukshetra*, August, p. 63.

Kanango, Sukla Deb (1996), "Panchayati Raj and Emerging Women Leadership: An Overview", *Social Action*, Vol. 46.

Kaushik, Anupma and Gayatri Shaktawat (2010), "Women in Panchayati Raj Institutions: A Case Study of Chittorgarh District Council", *Journal of Developing Societies*, Vol. 26, No. 4, pp. 473-483.

Kaushik, S. (1993), "Women and Panchayati Raj", Har Anand Publications, New Delhi.

Kaushik, Susheela (1993), "Women and Panchayati Raj", *Indian Journal of Rural Development*.

Kerala Institute of Local Administration (2001), "Report of the Operational Level Training for Gram Panchayat Functionaries", Thrissur, Kerala, Kerala Institute of Local Administration.

Kishwar, M. (2000), "Equality of Opportunities vs. Equality of Results: Improving Women's Reservation Bill", *Economic and Political Weekly*, Vol. 35, No. 47, pp. 4151-4156.

Kishwar, M. (1996), "Women and Politics: Beyond Quota", *Economic and Political Weekly*, October 26, p. 2892.

Kishwar, M. (1988), "Nature of Women's Mobilization in Rural India: An Exploratory Essay", *Economic and Political Weekly*, Vol. 23, No. 52/53, December, pp. 2754-2763.

Krishna, Sudhir (1997), "Women and Panchayati Raj: The Law, Programme and Practices", *Journal of Rural Development*, Vol. 16(4), NIRD, Hyderabad, pp. 651-662.

Kudva, Neema (2003), "Engineering Elections: The Experiences of Women in Panchayati Raj in Karnataka", *International Journal of Politics, Culture, and Society*, Vol. 16, No. 3, Spring, pp. 445-463.

Kumud, Sharma (1998), "Transformative Politics: Dimensions of Women's Participation in Panchayati Raj", *Indian Journal of Gender Studies*, Vol. 5(1), Sage Publications, New Delhi.

Kurein, C.T. (1992), "Growth and Justice", Oxford University Press, Madras.

Lakshi, P. (1993), "Women and Politics: A Study in Political Participation", Book Link Corporation, Hyderabad.

Lal, Shiv Kumar (2007), "A Study of Issues and Challenges in Empowerment of Women through Their Participation in the Panchayat Raj Institution: A Case Study of Allahabad District of Uttar Pradesh", presented paper in National Level Seminar on Gender Issues and Empowerment of Women, Indian Statistical Institute, February 1-2, 2007.

Lindgren, Karl-Oskar, Magdalena Inkinen and Sten Widmalm (2009), "Who Knows Best What the People Want: Women or Men: A Study of Political Representation in India", *Comparative Political Studies*, Vol. 42, No. 1, pp. 31-55.

Madhya Pradesh Institute of Social Science Research (2001), "Operational Training for Gram Panchayat Officials, Ujjain: Madhya Pradesh Institute of Social Science Research.

Manikymba, P.P. (1989), "Women in Panchayati Raj: Promises and Performances", *Teaching Politics*, Vol. 14, pp. 3-4.

Manikymba, P. (1990), "Women Presiding Officer at the Tertiary Political Structure", *Journal of Rural Development*, Vol. 9(6).

Mehta Ashok (1979), "Report of the Committee on Panchayati Raj", Government of India, New Delhi.

Milbrath, W. Lester (1965), "Political Participation: How and When People Get Involved in Politics", Rand Mcnaly and Company, Chicago.

Mishra, S. (1995), "Women and Political Process in India", *Kurukeshtra*, Vol. XLIII, No. 2, August.

Mishra, Subrat (1995), "Orissa: Women and Economic Independence", *Social Action*, Vol. 45.

Mohanty, Bidyut (2002), "Women and Political Empowerment", ISS, New Delhi.

Mohanty, Bidyut (1995), "Panchayati Raj, 73rd Constitutional Amendment and Women", *Economic and Political Weekly*, Vol. 30, No. 52, December, pp. 3346-3350.

Mukherjee, Amitava (1995), "Participatory Rural Appraisal: Methods and Applications in Rural Planning", Vikas Publishing House, New Delhi.

Mukherjee, Neela (2002), "Participatory Learning and Action: With 100 Field Methods", Concept Publishing Company, New Delhi.

Mukherji, Nirmala (1993), "The Third Stratum", *Economic and Political Weekly*, May, pp. 854-862.

Narayan, Usha (1996), "Women in Panchayats: The Path Ahead", *Mainstream*, November 16.

National Institute of Rural Development (1994), "Training Modules for Panchayati Raj Functionaries", NIRD, Hyderabad.

Omeo, Kumar Das (2002), Institute of Social Change and Development, Modules for training programmes for PRIs of Tripura.

Ommen, John (1991), "Developing Women at Grassroots", *Kurukshetra*, February, pp. 40-42.

Panda, Snehalata (1995), "Gender, Environment and Participation in Politics", M.D. Publication, New Delhi.

Panda, Snehalata (1996), "Emerging Pattern of Leadership Among Rural Women in Orissa", *Indian Journal of Public Administration*, Vol. 42, No. 3-4.

Panda, Snehalata (1999), "Political Empowerment of Women: Case of Orissa Panchayati Raj Institutions", *Indian Journal of Public Administration*, Vol. 45.

Pandey, Saroj (1992), "Women's Education and Development in Orissa", *Social Change*, Vol. 22.

Participation and Governance Institute (2003), Report on One day Orientation Programme for Newly Elected Representatives, Nainital.

Pillai, Sudha (2001), "Can Panchayati Raj Improve the Scene?", *Yojana*, August.

Purushotam, Sangetha (1999), "Empowerment of Women in India: Grassroots Women's Network and State", *Indian Journal of Public Administration*, Vol. 45.

Rajjeswari (no date), "Women's Participation in PRIs: A Case Study from Tamil Nadu", M.S Swaminathan Research Foundation., Chennai.

Ramachandra and Ramathilagam G. (1995), "The 73rd Constitutional Amendment and Its Implication for Women", *Kurukshetra*, Vol. XLIII, No. 7, April, pp. 94-97.

Ramaswamy, Sushila (2005), "India's Crisis of Governance: The Women's Perspective", *Policy and Society*, Vol. 24, Issue 3, pp. 122-141.

Reddy, T.C. (1989), "Rural Leadership: Continuity and Change", *Indian Journal of Social Research*, Vol. 30:4, p. 389.

Saxena, Kiran (1994), "Empowerment of Women: The Indian Context", *Indian Journal of Public Administration*, Vol. 55.

Saxena, N.C. (2000), "Note on What is Meant by People's Participation", *Journal of Rural Development*.

Sharma, Kumud (1987), "Women in Struggle", Occasional monograph, Centre for Women's Development Studies, New Delhi.

Sodhi, J.S. and M.S. Ramanujam (2006), "Panchayati Raj System: A Study in Five States of India, *Indian Journal of Industrial Relations*, Vol. 42, No. 1, July, pp. 1-41.

Srinivas, M.N. (1978), "The Changing Position of Indian Women", Oxford University Press, New Delhi.

"State of Panchayats, 2007-08: An Independent Assessment", Vol. 1, Institute of Rural Management, Anand (IRMA) with the Ministry of Panchayati Raj, Government of India, New Delhi.

Stephen, F. (2001), "Empowering Women in Panchayats through Training in Building Women's Capacities", in Interventions in Gender Transformations, (ed.), Ranjini K. Murthy, Sage Publications India, New Delhi.

Task Force on Panchayati Raj, Rajiv Gandhi Foundation (2003), "Empowering Panchayats: Handbook for Master Trainers (Using Participatory Approach)", Concept Publishing Co., New Delhi.

Tiwari, Nupur (2009), "Rethinking the Rotation Term of Reservation in Panchayats", *Economic and Political Weekly*, January.

V. Annamali (1994), "Emergency Structure of Panchayat Raj in India: A Comparative Analysis of New Acts of States", *Indian Journal of Public Administration*, Vol. XL, October-December, No.4.

Vijayalakshmi, V. (2008), "Rent-Seeking and Gender in Local Governance", *Journal of Development Studies*, October, Vol. 44, No. 9, pp. 1262-1288.

Widmalm, Sten (2005), "Explaining Corruption at the Village and Individual Level in India: Findings from a Study of the Panchayati Raj Reforms", *Asian Survey*, Vol. 45, No. 5, September-October, pp. 756-776.

Index

Index